IMAGES
of America

BOSTON
ORGANIZED CRIME

ON THE COVER: John Burke and Frank Karlonas were handcuffed together and photographed inside this police paddy wagon in 1933. Karlonas and Burke were being held as suspects in the murder of Charles "King" Solomon, a popular nightclub owner from the Prohibition era who was a reputed bootlegger and "rum lord." Solomon was gunned down at Boston's Cotton Club on January 24, 1933. Karlonas and Burke were ultimately acquitted. (Courtesy of the Boston Public Library, Leslie Jones Collection.)

IMAGES
of America

BOSTON
ORGANIZED CRIME

Emily Sweeney

ARCADIA
PUBLISHING

Published by Arcadia Publishing
Charleston, South Carolina

Printed in the United States of America

Library of Congress Control Number: 2011933823

For all general information, please contact Arcadia Publishing:
Telephone 843-853-2070
Fax 843-853-0044
E-mail sales@arcadiapublishing.com
For customer service and orders:
Toll-Free 1-888-313-2665

Visit us on the Internet at www.arcadiapublishing.com

*This book is dedicated to the victims and their friends and families,
and anyone else who has been affected by violent crime.*

CONTENTS

ACKNOWLEDGMENTS

This book would not have been possible without the help and support of so many people. I would like to especially thank Officer Scott Wilder of the Brookline Police Department; David Dahl, Janice Page, Wanda Joseph-Rollins, Kim Tan, Dean Inouye, George Rizer, Dave Morrow, and the rest of my colleagues at the *Boston Globe*; Diane Wiffin at the Massachusetts Department of Correction; Gregory J. Comcowich and Michelle Goldschen at the FBI; David Procopio of the Massachusetts State Police; David Boeri; Erin Rocha, Ryan Easterling, and Lissie Cain at Arcadia Publishing; Jane Winton and Tom Blake of the Boston Public Library; and Bob Cullum, for generously allowing me to use so many photographs from his grandfather's photograph collection. I would also like to thank my friends and family—especially Jeannie Sweeney-Rock, Ed Rock, Charlie Sweeney, and Bob Sweeney—for putting up with me while I wrote and researched this book and Katie Hunt, for keeping me on track and letting me take over her desk to (finally!) finish this project.

INTRODUCTION

Boston has long been a hub for organized crime in New England. Of course, criminals are not confined by municipal boundary lines. Many gangsters who ruled Boston's streets retreated to quiet, tree-lined roads and big mansions in tony suburbs to get their sleep. Around Boston's periphery, nearby cities like Revere and Somerville had cultivated their own homegrown gangs and underworld networks. As Revere police chief Philip Gallo told the *Boston Globe* in 1967, loan sharks were coming out to Revere to party "because this is where the action is. Revere isn't a bedroom town. We can't put a fence around the place and say 'stay out.'"

So the title of this book—*Boston Organized Crime*—is slightly misleading. It actually covers a much larger geography. These photographs provide a glimpse into shady corners and back alleys all over the Greater Boston area—places where deals were made, alliances were broken, and people were executed in cold blood.

The first images in this collection are from the Prohibition Era, a time when organized crime really began to take root in Boston. After the sale of alcoholic beverages was banned in 1920, the booze business went underground and flourished illegally. Enterprising criminals set up secret stills and speakeasies. Bootleggers and rumrunners ruled the day, stepping up to meet the demand of quenching the public's thirst for beer and liquor. It was a profitable industry, one that created much wealth for those in the nightlife and entertainment business. It was during this time that powerful figures like Charles "King" Solomon emerged.

Prohibition provided plenty of opportunities for thieves and thugs to reap big profits. One of the most notorious was the Gustin Gang of South Boston, a band of hoodlums who became known for committing robberies, hijacking liquor trucks, and roughing up police officers.

After Prohibition was repealed, and alcoholic beverages became legal again, Boston area criminals continued to make money from other illicit endeavors. Gambling was one market that they cornered early on. Betting pools, poker games, and horse races were big business back in the days before the state-run lottery. A federal survey estimated that $90 million had been taken in Massachusetts by number pool and horse-betting promoters in the 1930s, which meant that the state had been defrauded of $1.5 million in income taxes. In the decades to come, illegal gambling continued to thrive in the Bay State, with bookmaking luminaries such as Harry "Doc" Sagansky and Joseph "Hoodsie" Hotze leading the way. Illegal gaming was a local institution. One Justice Department official, marveling at the size of the operations here, remarked: "The numbers racket in Boston has been established to a degree that doesn't exist anywhere else in the country."

All of this under-the-radar, off-the-books money-making activity set the backdrop for violent crime. Police investigators were stymied by the eerie code of silence on the street. At times, fear and intimidation seemed to prevail. In September 1943, Municipal Court judge Elijah Adlow expressed his frustration in court, when he bristled at the faulty memories of people who supposedly witnessed a bloody shooting at the Latin Quarter nightclub. "People won't come into court and tell the truth . . . They are afraid to come in here. They're afraid of their lives," said Adlow. "A few tough guys have got this town in a reign of terror. They run the town."

Organized crime in Boston really rose to prominence in the 1960s, when the Mafia became the talk of the town. In 1963, several underworld figures in New England were accused of being part of a broad, nationwide crime syndicate known as Cosa Nostra, which roughly translates to "our thing" in Italian. (Today, the FBI refers to the Mafia as La Cosa Nostra, or LCN, for short.) In US Senate hearings, Raymond L. S. Patriarca, a Worcester native who lived in Providence,

Rhode Island, was identified as the boss of the New England mob. FBI director J. Edgar Hoover called out Gennaro "Jerry" Angiulo, of Boston's North End, as being Patriarca's top lieutenant.

The feds set their sights on taking down the Mafia, and a wiretap was set up at Patriarca's office in Providence in March 1962. Another microphone was planted at Jay's Lounge, at 255 Tremont Street in Boston, so they could eavesdrop on Jerry Angiulo's conversations. And through the FBI's Top Echelon Criminal Informant Program, federal agents recruited local underworld figures into squealing on their brethren. (Stephen J. "The Rifleman" Flemmi, his brother "Jimmy the Bear" Flemmi, and James "Whitey" Bulger were among the informants they depended on.)

As the feds waged their war against the Italian Mafia, another war was unfolding on the streets of Greater Boston. An epic feud between the McLaughlin brothers of Charlestown and Buddy McLean of Somerville resulted in so many murders that observers were left wondering if crime in Boston was really organized at all. In February 1967, *Life* magazine ran a double-page spread showing the faces of 39 men who had been killed on the streets of Greater Boston. Above them, the headline said: "The thugs 'squash' each other, one by one VICTIMS." The growing body count in gangland seemed to prove that there was not any single entity running the show, at least not in Greater Boston. This was blood-spattered retribution, replayed over and over again.

Law enforcement was bolstered in the 1970s thanks to the federal Organized Crime Control Act, a new law that included the more widely known Racketeer Influenced and Corrupt Organizations Statute—commonly called "RICO"—which helped prosecutors put more mobsters behind bars. As the hoodlums involved in the so-called "Irish Gang Wars" of the 1960s died off, and others went to jail, power in local underworld thinned out and became more consolidated.

Unfortunately, it did not mark an end to violent crime. There were still gangland slayings, for various reasons. Turf battles. Betrayal. Revenge. Greed. Protection. A relentless pursuit for more money, more power. The fear of being snitched on and locked up in jail, or even worse—killed.

Boston Organized Crime highlights some of the low points in our local history. The photographs I chose to include in this book span almost a century—but it is far from being a complete photographic record of organized crime in the Greater Boston area. It is more like a sampling.

It would be impossible to capture the complete stories of the FBI agents, police officers, murder victims, and alleged assassins mentioned in this 128-page book. I was limited to writing brief captions for each photograph, so I tried to include the most relevant and interesting information that space would allow.

I also did my best to corroborate and cross-check every fact, figure, and anecdote cited in this book. I used several autobiographies as references and interviewed sources on both sides of the law. I sifted through old case files and flipped through musty manila folders filled with black and white photographs and yellowed newspaper clippings. I looked up old news articles and obituaries in the *Boston Globe* archives and read through stacks of court transcripts and documents. (To see some of the sources I used, check out the abbreviated bibliography on page 127). If anyone has any comments or suggestions about the material in this book, or anything I have written here, do not hesitate to contact me. You can reach me by visiting www.BostonOrganizedCrime.com.

And dear readers, please keep this in mind as you flip through these pages: this is a compilation of particular moments in time that were captured on film—many of which are violent and down-right disturbing. While there are lessons to be learned from these haunting images, we must remember that these are not just photographs of various murder victims and convicted criminals. These are people's fathers, grandfathers, uncles, sons, friends, and neighbors. They are not scenes from a movie. This is real life. And it is a part of our past that cannot be ignored. The mug shots and crime scene photographs contained in this book are pieces of history chronicling a violent past that we cannot—and should not—forget. They illustrate how criminality, human nature, and the community of Greater Boston have changed—and how much has stayed the same—over the years.

—Emily Sweeney

One

PROHIBITION DAYS

"Goofy Campbell" Guiffre was a gangster who lived in Boston's North End. After he was gunned down at a Hanover Street barbershop in January 1931, he was laid to rest in a $2,000 silver-gray casket, and his funeral featured six cars full of flowers and heavy police detail.. The Associated Press described it as "the first big-time gangland funeral this city has seen." (Courtesy of the Boston Public Library, Leslie Jones Collection.)

The 18th Amendment, which took effect in 1920, prohibited anyone from making, selling, or transporting alcoholic beverages. As a result, drinking went underground and criminal enterprises took over the production of booze. Above, Boston police superintendent Michael H. Crowley bends over to get a close-up view of a speakeasy on Tremont Street. Crowley took a hard line against gun-toting hoodlums and street violence. In August 1931, Crowley vowed: "We are going to take the offensive in Boston against gangland." More than once he instructed Boston officers to "shoot to kill." Below, Crowley shows off two handguns at police headquarters. (Both, courtesy of the Boston Public Library, Leslie Jones Collection.)

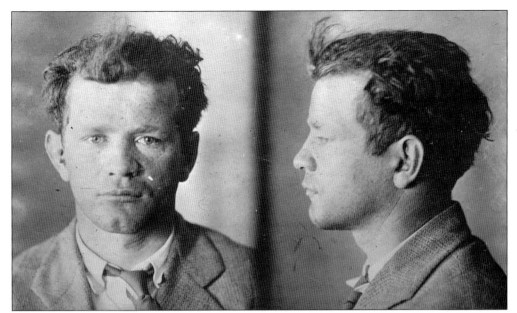

The Gustin Gang was one of Boston's most notorious gangs of the Prohibition era. Their name came from Gustin Street in South Boston, and most of them were Irish. Authorities identified former boxer Stephen J. Wallace (above) and his brother Frank (below) as the leaders of this outlaw group. Newspapers at the time referred to them as Steve and Frankie Gustin. (Courtesy of the Boston Public Library, Leslie Jones Collection.)

Frankie Wallace was soft-spoken, mild-mannered, and always getting into trouble. He made national headlines in 1928 when he was accused of taking part in a hold-up robbery of the *Detroit News*. Over the course of his criminal career, he was arrested 25 times but only did jail time twice, serving two short sentences at Deer Island in 1919 and 1928. (Courtesy of the Boston Public Library, Leslie Jones Collection.)

Frankie Wallace met his untimely death on December 22, 1931, while visiting a rival gang's headquarters in Boston's North End. Wallace and two other Gustin gangsters—Timothy J. Coffey and Bernard "Dodo" Walsh—had gone over to Joseph Lombardo's office at 317 Hanover Street to talk business. They walked up to Lombardo's business on the third floor, C.F. Importers, and then bullets started flying. Coffey ran down the hallway into Julius H. Wolfson's law office (highlighted by the arrow), where he crouched behind a screen and protected himself with a chair. Wallace staggered in after him and slumped over another chair, bleeding. He had been shot in the back. Betty Franklin, the office stenographer, screamed and hid underneath her desk. (Courtesy of the Boston Public Library, Leslie Jones Collection.)

Bernard "Dodo" Walsh (right) was near the stairwell when he was hit by a .38-caliber bullet. He tumbled down the stairs and died facedown on the second-floor landing. Walsh was 24 years old and had lived on Adams Street in Dorchester. Timothy J. Coffey managed to survive the ambush but later refused to testify about the incident. He also ended his ties with the Gustin Gang. (Courtesy of the Boston Public Library, Leslie Jones Collection.)

Police investigators surveyed the damage in Wolfson's office after the shoot-out at 317 Hanover Street. One of the gunmen had thrown a pistol through the glass window behind Betty Franklin, the office stenographer. It had crashed through the glass and landed on the sidewalk below. (Courtesy of the Boston Public Library, Leslie Jones Collection.)

Authorities inspect some of the guns that were seized from 317 Hanover Street. The 1931 slaying of Frankie Wallace and his so-called "henchman," Bernard Walsh, proved to be a turning point for organized crime in Boston—the Italian mob had put the Irish gangsters from South Boston in their place. On December 29, 1931, Boston police superintendent Michael H. Crowley released a wanted poster (below) for Joseph Lombardo, alias Lombardi. He stood five feet, eight inches tall and weighed 140 pounds. Boston police described him as a 35-year-old cloak maker with a dark complexion and maroon-colored eyes. The *Boston Globe* referred to him as a "North End bootleg leader." (Both, courtesy of the Boston Public Library, Leslie Jones Collection.)

51974 POLICE DEPARTMENT, BOSTON, MASS. FORMULA

WANTED FOR MURDER

| 1. RIGHT THUMB | 2. RIGHT INDEX | 3. RIGHT MIDDLE | 4. RIGHT RING | 5. RIGHT LITTLE |
| 6. LEFT THUMB | 7. LEFT INDEX | 8. LEFT MIDDLE | 9. LEFT RING | 10. LEFT LITTLE |

JOSEPH LOMBARDI, alias LOMBARDO
(Picture taken 1925)

DESCRIPTION: Age 35 years; height 5 feet 8 inches; weight 140 pounds; complexion dark; eyes maroon; hair chestnut black; build medium; occupation cloak maker.

We hold warrant for Joseph Lombardo, alias Lombardo, for murder, December 22, 1931, by shooting Bernard Walsh and Frank Wallace.

Arrest, hold and wire at my expense.

MICHAEL H. CROWLEY,
Superintendent.

December 29, 1931.

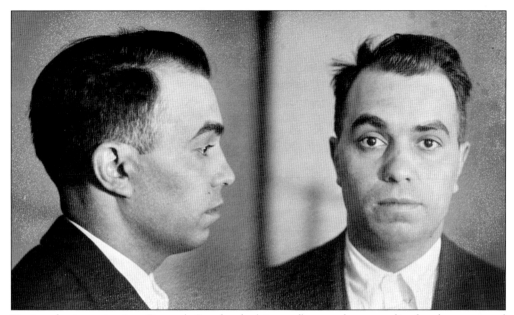

During the investigation, Pasquale Lombardo (pictured) was taken to police headquarters and questioned about his brother Joseph's whereabouts. Joseph Lombardo eventually turned himself in, on New Year's Eve. Wearing a brown fedora, his coat collar turned up and a bodyguard at his side, the suspected mob boss strolled into the police station and coolly declined to answer any questions. (Courtesy of the Boston Public Library, Leslie Jones Collection.)

Frankie Wallace's wake was held at his family's home at 1744 Columbia Road in South Boston on December 26, 1931. He was buried in New Calvary Cemetery in Mattapan. A crowd gathered outside of the house on the day of his funeral. Over 200 vehicles—many with license plates from outside of New England—were in the funeral cortege for the slain Gustin Gang leader, and six cars were filled with flowers. (Photograph by Emily Sweeney.)

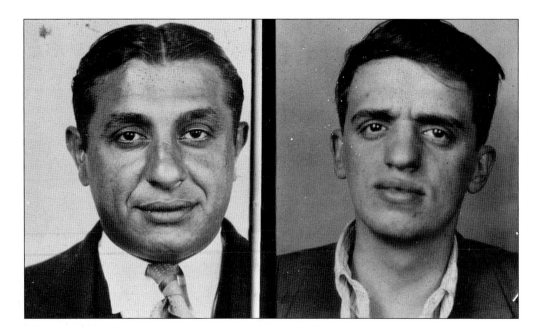

Henry Selvitella (above, left) and Anthony W. Cortese (above, right) were also picked up and questioned about the shoot-out at 317 Hanover Street. Selvitella (also known as Henry Noyes and Henry Selvitelli) lived in the North End and was known to police as a "leading figure in the rackets." Cortese was allegedly his gun-toting bodyguard. Born in August 1909, Cortese (below) once lived at 23 Snow Hill Street in the North End of Boston. He stood five feet, nine inches tall and weighed 250 pounds, and on the streets he was known as "Big Bozo." (Above, courtesy of the Boston Public Library, Leslie Jones Collection; below, courtesy of the Brookline Police Department.)

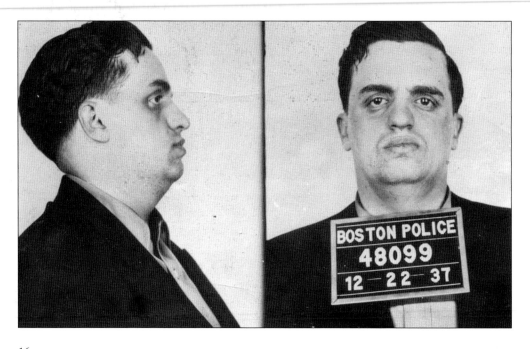

A few days after the shoot-out, police nabbed Cortese and Selvitella at a shoeshine parlor on Hanover Street where Selvitella was getting his shoes shined. The arresting officer approached Selvitella first and said, "I want you." And Selvitella replied, "I expected that." At the time, Cortese was armed with three loaded revolvers. The murder charges went nowhere, but Cortese ended up getting busted for carrying concealed weapons. He was sentenced to serve up to three and a half years in state prison. It was not Cortese's first brush with the law, nor would it be his last. (Courtesy of the Brookline Police Department.)

Steve Wallace (also known as Gustin) was accused of severely beating a Boston police officer on January 15, 1933. It all started inside this brick home at 2 Vinton Street in South Boston, which was a speakeasy in the 1930s. That evening, at around 6:30 p.m., Officer Daniel J. McDonald showed up in plainclothes and drank some whiskey in the company of the Gustin Gang. (Photograph by Emily Sweeney.)

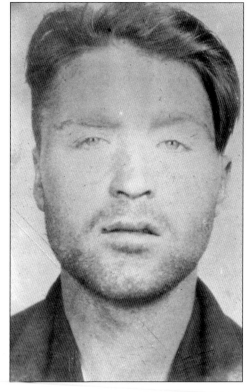

One of the men at the speakeasy, Thomas G. "Red" Curran (right), would later turn government witness and testify that Steve Wallace spiked McDonald's drink. After McDonald was knocked out, Curran said members of the Gustin Gang threw McDonald down a flight of stairs, kicked him out onto the street, beat him with a hammer, and left the unconscious officer in a field off D Street. (Courtesy of the Boston Public Library, Leslie Jones Collection.)

Soon after he testified about the McDonald beating, Thomas G. "Red" Curran turned up dead. In May 1933, his bullet-riddled body was found in this old quarry in West Quincy. He had been shot and then placed inside a car that was pushed over a rocky cliff into the water below. (Courtesy of the Boston Public Library, Leslie Jones Collection.)

On May 28, 1933, Curran's body was pulled out of the water and brought up to a wooden landing so Boston police officers could get a closer look and confirm his identity. He was dressed in a tuxedo and had been shot five times in the head, arms, and chest.

Very few people attended Curran's funeral on June 1, 1933. A group of women stopped by the undertaking parlor at 906 Dorchester Avenue to pay their respects that morning, but they did not stay long. The service consisted of Boston police sergeant James V. Crowley reciting the rosary, and that was it. This is what the building at 906 Dorchester Avenue looks like today. (Photograph by Emily Sweeney.)

Curran was laid to rest at Mount Hope Cemetery in Mattapan. Like his funeral, the burial was sparsely attended; none of his relatives or friends showed up. The only people present were a handful of Boston police officers. (Courtesy of the Boston Public Library, Leslie Jones Collection.)

Two days later, huge crowds gathered to watch authorities lift the "Curran murder car" from the depths of the quarry. A diver ventured deep into the dark waters to attach a chain and steel cable to the 1933 blue sedan. Hundreds of people—including police officers armed with riot guns—looked on as the vehicle was slowly raised out of the water. (Courtesy of the Boston Public Library, Leslie Jones Collection.)

Wanted on charges of beating a police officer, Stevie Gustin avoided capture until the summer of 1933, when three Boston police officers in a taxi spotted him leaning against a lamppost in New York City's Times Square. After spending five months on the lam, the 32-year-old Wallace returned to Boston in shackles. He was later tried and found not guilty of murderous assault on Officer Daniel J. McDonald. (Courtesy of the Boston Public Library, Leslie Jones Collection.)

After Wallace was acquitted in December 1933, a new indictment came down, charging him with conspiring to kill Officer McDonald. Wallace disappeared again, and he remained on the loose until he surrendered to police on October 29, 1934. Capt. Stephen J. Flaherty (below, left) and Det. William J. Crowley (below, right) picked up Wallace at Old Harbor Street in South Boston. This time he was convicted and sentenced to serve two and a half years at Deer Island. (Courtesy of the Boston Public Library, Leslie Jones Collection.)

Two

KILLING KING SOLOMON

Charles "King" Solomon was a popular nightclub owner—known to police as a "rum lord"—who allegedly ran a multimillion-dollar liquor-and-narcotics bootlegging syndicate. Polite, well mannered, and charming, Solomon owned nightclubs, theaters, hotels, and restaurants, including the infamous Cocoanut Grove nightclub, where he is pictured at right. He was known to feds as "the Capone of the East." (Courtesy of the Boston Public Library, Leslie Jones Collection.)

Solomon was a social butterfly who was not afraid to flaunt his riches. He was a Russian immigrant who once worked behind the counter of a restaurant, serving lunch to local newsboys. He emerged from that modest, working-class background as a powerful and wealthy businessman. (Courtesy of the Boston Public Library, Leslie Jones Collection.)

Gangsters at Boston's Cotton Club shot Solomon to death in the early morning on January 24, 1933. This photograph shows the exterior of the club, which was located at 892–894 Tremont Street in the Roxbury section of the city, next door to Sweet's Market. (Courtesy of the Boston Public Library, Leslie Jones Collection.)

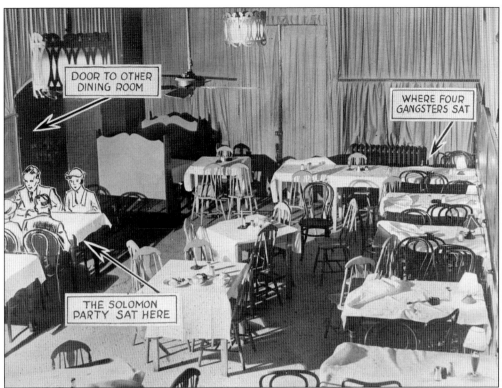

On that fateful night, after business ended at the Cocoanut Grove, Solomon tucked $4,600 into his pocket and invited two dancers to visit the Cotton Club with him. Solomon's chauffeur drove them over to the club, where they were joined by the Cocoanut Grove's orchestra leader. At one point during the evening, "King" Solomon went to the men's washroom, where he was shot. Afterward, he reportedly gasped: "Those dirty rats—got me!" The photograph below shows the back alley behind the Cotton Club, where the murderers might have escaped. (Both, courtesy of the Boston Public Library, Leslie Jones Collection.)

Solomon was rushed to Boston City Hospital, where boxing promoter Dan Carroll joined him at his bedside. Solomon never identified his killers. On his death certificate, his occupation was listed as "theatre owner." He was 46 years old and lived at 193 Fuller Street in Brookline. The cause of death was pistol shot wounds to the arm, chest, and abdomen. On February 2, 1933, police located the alleged getaway car (above) used by the King Solomon murder suspects; it had been abandoned in a wooded area in South Foxborough (below). (Both, courtesy of the Boston Public Library, Leslie Jones Collection.)

News of King Solomon's death made headlines. As shown above, reporters rushed over to Boston's Cotton Club to interview police and ask questions about the murder investigation. Solomon's funeral was held on January 26, 1933. Flowers filled the rooms of Solomon's house in Brookline, where the wake was held. A *Boston Globe* reporter stood among the 3,000 spectators gathered at the corner of Abbotsford Road and Fuller Street. He described the scene as a mixed crowd of cops, reporters, photographers, lawyers, actresses, "small fry racketeers," and "little Caesars of gangland, who kept their right hands in right-hand pockets and answered questions with the word 'Scram!'" Visitors to the house included boxing promoter Dan Carroll, Cotton Club owner Tommy Maren, and noted gambler and club owner David "Beano" Breen. (Both, courtesy of the Boston Public Library, Leslie Jones Collection.)

King Solomon was under indictment when he was murdered. But despite his reputation for partaking in questionable enterprises, he did not have a lengthy criminal record. The only time he spent behind bars was after he was convicted of subornation of perjury in January 1923 and sentenced to five years in federal prison—he served 13 months and was released early. (Courtesy of the Boston Public Library, Leslie Jones Collection.)

Solomon was buried at the Hand-in-Hand Jewish Cemetery in West Roxbury. The funeral procession included three cars and two hearses filled with floral tributes. More than 500 people followed Solomon's casket through the cemetery. Throngs of people walked across graves and navigated around tombstones to see Boston's nightlife "King" laid to rest for good. (Courtesy of the Boston Public Library, Leslie Jones Collection.)

Michael J. "Spike" Hennessey was questioned by police and placed in a lineup at Station 10 in Roxbury. He told officers that he was not anywhere near the Cotton Club on the night Solomon was killed and he did not know who did it. Had he been involved with the shooting, Hennessey said: "I would have been on my way to another climate." (Courtesy of the Boston Public Library, Leslie Jones Collection.)

Authorities charged James H. Scully, John T. O'Donnell, John J. Burke, James "Skeets" Coyne, and Frank Karlonas in connection with Solomon's murder. Newspapers referred to them as the "Cotton Club Killers." This photograph shows suspect O'Donnell flanked by Sgt. John J. McArdle (left) and Inspector Stanley Slack (right). (Courtesy of the Boston Public Library, Leslie Jones Collection.)

John J. Burke and Frank Karlonas were apprehended in New Orleans in April 1933. They arrived at Back Bay Station dressed in their summer clothes. Pictured above are, from left to right, Capt. Stephen J. Flaherty, Lt. Inspector John McCarthy, Karlonas, Burke, and Sgt. William J. McCarthy. Karlonas wears a straw hat and has a cigarette dangling from his lips, while Burke holds a newspaper and uses his hat to shield his eyes. At the time, Karlonas (below) was 24 years old and living on West Third Street in South Boston. Burke was 29, from Charlestown. Both denied any involvement in Solomon's murder. (Both, courtesy of the Boston Public Library, Leslie Jones Collection.)

Ellen Chase was dating John T. O'Donnell at the time. She told police that O'Donnell confessed to her that he was at the Cotton Club that night but did not participate in any shooting. O'Donnell told her that he was already on his way out of the club, and "Skeets" Coyne was alone with Solomon in the washroom when the shots were fired. (Courtesy of the Boston Public Library, Leslie Jones Collection.)

John Burke (right), Karlonas, and O'Donnell were tried first. At the end of the trial, the defendants waited nervously as the foreman read the verdict. When the verdict of "not guilty" was announced, the three young men smiled and appeared relieved. Burke loosened his tie as he looked around the courtroom for his friends and relatives. He was a free man. (Courtesy of the Boston Public Library, Leslie Jones Collection.)

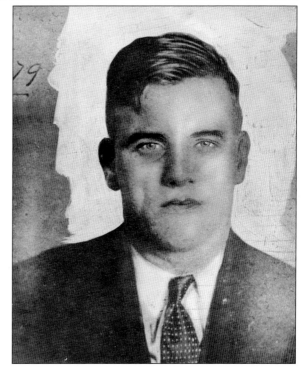

James "Skeets" Coyne was apprehended in Michigan City, Indiana. Coyne is pictured smoking a cigar with Capt. Stephen J. Flaherty (left) and Sgt. William J. McCarthy (right) at Roxbury Crossing Station in 1934. Coyne was an ex-con and former teamster and had once worked as a doorman at the Cotton Club. He later pleaded guilty to manslaughter and robbery charges and was sentences to 10–20 years. (Courtesy of the Boston Public Library, Leslie Jones Collection.)

James Scully (center) was arrested on October 24, 1933, while he was eating breakfast at an Upham's Corner restaurant in Dorchester. The former boxer denied being in the Cotton Club washroom when Solomon was shot. Scully was eventually convicted of robbing Solomon on the night he was killed and sentenced to 16 to 20 years in prison. (Courtesy of the Boston Public Library, Leslie Jones Collection.)

Three

Gambling, Robberies, and Rackets

On July 29, 1932, Boston police burst into a conference room on the 15th floor of the Hotel Manger. The men attending the closed-door meeting were suspected of running a lottery ring. Twenty-six men were taken into custody, including Joseph Lombardi, Frank Cucchiara, Philip Bruccola, and an up-and-coming 34-year-old bookmaker who identified himself as Harry Jasper. (Author's collection.)

In January 1943, Dr. Harry J. "Doc" Sagansky (also known as Doc Jasper) was among 23 suspects accused of being part of a multimillion-dollar number pool and horse race racket. He was 46 years old at the time. State police and federal agents raided several places and searched Sagansky's home, at 168 Gardner Road in Brookline, where they found pool slips in a locked closet. (Courtesy of the Massachusetts Department of Correction.)

On March 23, 1932, police seized 2,000 betting slips from a suspected bookmaking operation at 1 Boylston Street. While they searched the suite of offices, six telephones kept ringing—the callers were customers trying to place bets on horse races across the country. Officers answered the phones and politely took down their information. (Courtesy of the Boston Public Library, Leslie Jones Collection.)

 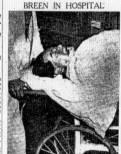

On December 17, 1937, David J. "Beano" Breen was shot while in the lobby of the Hotel Metropolitan, located at 315 Tremont Street. The 41-year-old former boxer ran a speakeasy at 358A Tremont Street and was known in the newspapers as a "racket boss." He lived with his wife just around the corner at 12 Melrose Street, in Boston's South End, and had recently started running a "strike-breaking" agency. When police asked Breen who shot him, he would not say—he just shrugged his shoulders, smiled, and said "cut it out." (Above, courtesy of the *Boston Globe*; right, author's collection.)

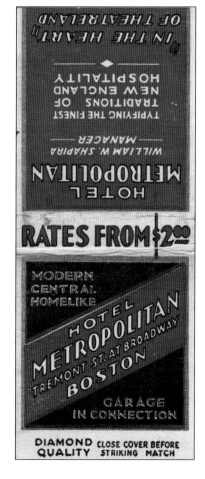

On January 31, 1949, Robert B. Holmes was shot at the Hotel Bostonian, located at 1138 Boylston Street. The reputed gangster staggered out a side door, bleeding, and then went missing for 10 days. His body was found leaning against the door of Revere Memorial Hospital on February 9. Police said the 36-year-old ex-convict had held up dice games in the past. They believed revenge might have been the motive. (Author's collection.)

On March 26, 1943, Joseph "Joe Beans" Palladino, 44, of Medford, and Joseph Guerriro, 42, of the North End, were shot inside the Latin Quarter nightclub. They both survived, but both gave different stories to police and claimed they did not know who shot them. At the time, Palladino was under indictment for his alleged involvement in "Doc" Sagansky's alleged $90-million numbers pool racket. (Author's collection.)

On January 17, 1950, one of the most famous holdups in history took place in Boston's North End. A group of masked men held up a Brink's security firm that was located inside this building, which borders Prince, Commercial, and Hull Streets. The robbers entered at 165 Prince Street. Brink's employees told authorities that the masked robbers were wearing Navy pea coats, gloves, and chauffeur caps. FBI investigators also learned that the thieves wore rubbers to muffle their footsteps as they made off with $1.2 million in cash and $1.5 million in checks, money orders, and securities. The press called it the "biggest robbery ever" and the "crime of the century." The 1978 film *The Brink's Job* was based on the story of the brazen heist. (Both photographs by Emily Sweeney.)

WANTED BY THE FBI

UNLAWFUL FLIGHT TO AVOID PROSECUTION (ARMED ROBBERY)

Photograph taken November 1941

THOMAS FRANCIS RICHARDSON

with aliases: James Gately, Thomas Kendricks, Patrick T. Nash, Thomas Richards, Thomas W. Richardson, "Sandy"

DESCRIPTION

Age 48, born March 22, 1907, Boston, Massachusetts (not verified); Height, 5'7" to 5'8½"; Weight, 140-145 pounds; Build, medium; Hair, gray; Eyes, blue; Complexion, ruddy; Race, white; Nationality, American; Occupation, longshoreman; Scars and marks, scar on left side of head; Remarks, may be wearing rimless eyeglasses, has a full upper

Thomas F. Richardson was charged with fleeing the state of Massachusetts to avoid being prosecuted for the Brink's robbery. The FBI issued this wanted flyer in January 1956. It described Richardson as a chain-smoking longshoreman with a "noticeably hoarse voice" and "a habit of losing false teeth when drinking." He was added to the FBI's 10 Most Wanted list in April 1956 and was later arrested, with James Faherty, on May 16, 1956. (Courtesy of the Federal Bureau of Investigation.)

James Ignatius Faherty was added to the FBI's 10 Most Wanted list in 1956. Authorities finally caught him hiding out in a Dorchester apartment on May 16, 1956. In August 1956, Faherty, Richardson, and six other men—Anthony Pino, Adolph "Jazz" Maffie, Joe McGinnis, Vincent Costa, Henry Baker, and Michael Geagan—were tried for the Brink's robbery. They were all found guilty and sentenced to life in prison. (Courtesy of the Federal Bureau of Investigation.)

John F. "Fats" Buccelli was a Boston underworld figure who was murdered in 1958. The *Boston Globe* described the 44-year-old as a "hulking mobster." His body was found inside a sedan that had crashed into a parked truck at Chandler and Arlington Streets, in Boston's South End. He had been shot twice in the head. Buccelli had served jail time on Deer Island in 1956 for receiving $57,000 in cash from the Brink's robbery. (Courtesy of the Massachusetts Department of Correction.)

John J. Buccelli   S.P.# 21461

Height: 5' 6"   Weight: 222 lbs.

Hair: Dk. Brown   Eyes: Dk. Hazel

Complexion: Dark

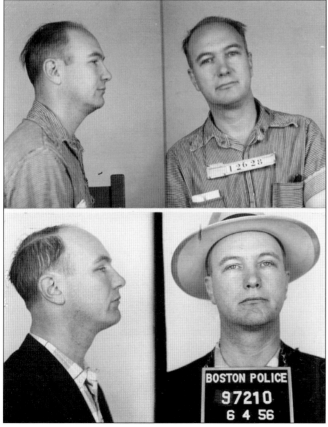

Edward A. "Wimpy" Bennett also served a one-year term on Deer Island with Fats Buccelli for receiving $57,000 of the Brink's loot. Bennett was once described by police as the most powerful influence in Boston's underworld, outside of the Mafia. His turf included Dorchester, Roxbury, and Somerville. (Courtesy of the Massachusetts State Police.)

Morris "Whitey" Hurwitz was a blond-haired, blue-eyed Jewish boxer who got caught up in the dark side of the underworld. Hurwitz's longshoreman ID card, which was issued to him on May 22, 1944, is pictured here. At the time, he was 32 years old; stood five feet, seven inches tall; and weighed 180 pounds. (Courtesy of the Brookline Police Department.)

Hurwitz is pictured here with the 1935 world heavyweight champion, Jimmy Braddock (center), and Jack McCarthy (left), Braddock's friend and sparring partner. Hurwitz traveled to Chicago to be in McCarthy's corner when he fought on the same card with Braddock on June 22, 1937—the day Braddock was defeated by Joe Louis. The 2005 movie *Cinderella Man* was based on Braddock's life. (Courtesy of the Brookline Police Department.)

The photograph at right shows Morris "Whitey" Hurwitz in happier times, enjoying a sunny day at the beach. Those came to an end on January 6, 1953, when Hurwitz was shot in the head outside his home in Brookline. The first officer at the scene asked him what happened, but Hurwitz could not break the seal of blood on his lips to speak. (Both, courtesy of the Brookline Police Department.)

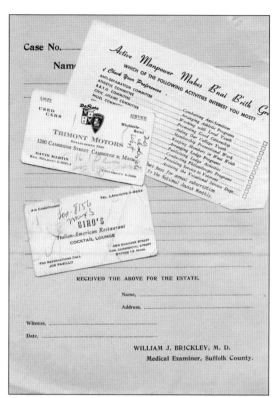

The night he was killed, Hurwitz was carrying a collegiate basketball schedule for that week—games that he would not live to see. He also carried business cards from Giro's, an Italian restaurant in Boston's North End that was known to be a favorite hangout for underworld characters. (Courtesy of the Brookline Police Department.)

In January 1956, the *Boston Globe* reported that Brink's robbery suspect Joseph "Specs" O'Keefe told authorities that Hurwitz had been killed by Elmer "Trigger" Burke. O'Keefe had a strong motive to blame Burke—two years earlier, Burke had tried gunning down O'Keefe in Dorchester. After testifying in the Brink's case, O'Keefe later moved to Hollywood, assumed a new identity, and worked as a chauffeur for Cary Grant. (Courtesy of the Brookline Police Department.)

Leo S. Swartz (pictured at right and below) and Thomas A. Callahan were also suspects in the Whitey Hurwitz murder case. Swartz was born in Boston in 1914, lived in Jamaica Plain, and listed his occupation as "salesman." He stood five feet, six inches tall and had brown eyes and brown hair. He was 38 years old. Both Callahan and Swartz were held and questioned by police and both denied any involvement. The *Boston Globe* reported that both men had alibis: Callahan told police he spent the night with his in-laws in Boston on the night of the murder, and Swartz said he was at home with his wife. After being questioned by police, both men were eventually freed. (Both, courtesy of the Brookline Police Department.)

Thomas A. Callahan (pictured at left and below) was well known to police. Over the years, he was charged with armed robbery, assault and battery, and other offenses. He was in and out of jail. On September 6, 1936, he made a sensational escape from the East Cambridge Jail that drew nationwide attention. The *Boston Globe* reported that Callahan broke away from standing in line with 108 prisoners, climbed up a drain pipe to a roof, dove headfirst through a window screen into an adjoining building, and jumped 15 feet from a window ledge to the street below, where he hopped into a getaway car that sped away. He was captured 11 months later in Fairview, New Jersey, for putting slugs into a telephone box; he told police his name was George Maguire. (Both, courtesy of the Brookline Police Department.)

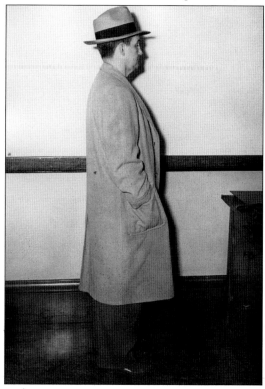

3955

TOWN OF BROOKLINE
POLICE DEPARTMENT
BROOKLINE, MASSACHUSETTS

RECORD SHEET

F.P.

NAME Thomas A. CALLAHAN, alias John F. BURKE, John T. BURKE

CROWLEY CRIME CLASSIFICATION

HISTORY FILE NO.

ADDRESS

PHOTO NO

DATE OF BIRTH 12/21/05 -Boston

DATE	OFFENSE	COURT	DISPOSITION
2/5/23	Dist. Peace	So.Boston	$50 appeal
3/22/23	Dist. Peace	Suf.Sup.	$25 paid
4/28/23	Larceny	B.P.D.	Probation
6/16/23	Drunkenness	So.Boston	Released
7/9/23	Larceny	Central	6 mos. H.C. appeal
10/4/23	Larceny	Suffolk Sup.	1 mo. H.C.
6/16/24	No Lic.	Dorchester	$20 fine
10/21/24	Robbery 2 cts.	Dorchester	B.O. to G.J.
3/20/25	Robbery	Suffolk Sup.	5 yrs. to Mass. Ref.
4/9/25	B & E d.t.	Suffolk Sup.	Filed
4/14/26	B & F N.T.	Suffolk Sup.	Filed
8/4/26	A & B	So. Boston	$25 fine
7/20/27	B & E	So. Boston	Waived Examination
7/22/27	Speed	Waltham	$20 paid
8/3/2	Att. B & E	Suffolk Sup.	No Bill
5/7/28	Larceny	Dorchester	B.O. for G.J.
8/10/28	Att.Robbery Jewelry Case	B.P.D.	Released
8/11/28	Larceny of Auto	Central	
8/23/28	S.P.	Phil. Pol.	Discharged
9/4/28	Dft. Rem. above 2 cts.	Central Ct.	
9/15/28	Reformatory Parole Rev.		
9/27/28	Ret. to Reformatory		
10/11/28	Rel.Habeas to State Prison for Suffolk		Sup. Ct.Larc. Auto 4½to5 S.P.
12/13/29	Transport to State Prison Colony		
12/18/30	Ret. to State Prison		
3/20/31	Transported to Rutland P.C.		
12/19/32	Paroled		
6/5/33	S.P.	B.P.D.	Released
11/9/33	Murder of Boston Police Officer		
3/3/36	To be returned to Boston	Prov. R.I.	
3/2/36	Destruction of Property		
	Fugitive from Justice	Prov. R.I.	
5/22 /36	Discharged by Executive Auth. to Mass.		Authorities
5/22/36	Murder		
6/16/36	No Probale Cause		
6/16/36	Robbery	Cambridge	
9/6/36	Escape from E.Cambridge Jail		Jail
8/11/37	Using slugs in coin box	Fairview,N.J.	Committed to Hackensack, N.J
8/13/37	E. Cambridge Jail Escape	Bail of $25,000.	
9/13/37	S.P. Armed Robbery		12-15 yrs. S.P.
	Escape from Jail 4-6 yrs. on & aft. above sentence		
1/2/41	Tranfer to S.P.C.		
12/12/46	Ret. S.P.		
1/28/50	Discharegd from S.P.		
12/12/51	Accessory before fact to murder		
	Assault & Battery with Dangerous weapon		Boston Pol.
	Sgt. Arthur Quinn Sta. #6		

PD 1M 5-43 A

Like many other criminals of this era, Thomas A. Callahan was known to use aliases. The Brookline Police Department knew him as John Burke. His lengthy criminal record began in 1923, when he was 17 years old. That year, he was busted for disturbing the peace, larceny, and drunkenness. He was later charged with the 1933 murder of John "Keeno" Keenan at the Club Chalet at 261 Tremont Street but was ultimately acquitted. (Courtesy of the Brookline Police Department.)

On March 10, 1954, police raided an apartment at 1471 Beacon Street in Brookline, where Morris J. Weinstein, Harry "Doc" Sagansky, and Eugene F. Wermuth were suspected of running an illegal gambling operation. At 4:03 p.m., Brookline police officer John J. Dwyer rang the bell, entered the building, and observed two men kneeling in the corner of the apartment, stuffing papers into a hole in the floor. Dwyer rushed over as the men were trying to shut the trapdoor. When Sagansky tried to block him, Officer Dwyer said, "Don't try anything or I'll wrap this crowbar around your neck." Police ended up seizing number pool slips and horse race tally sheets from the men. (Both, courtesy of the Brookline Police Department.)

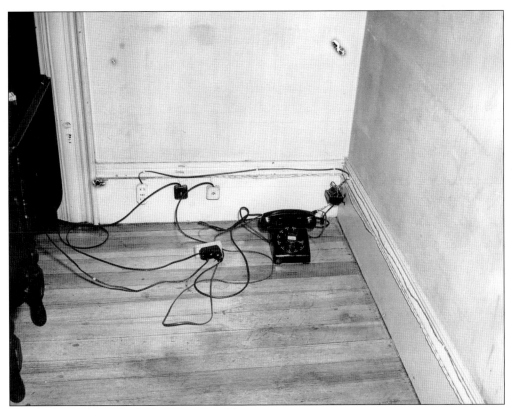

During the raid on March 10, 1954, a Brookline policeman photographed this telephone at 1471 Beacon Street. The telephone rang while police were searching for evidence, and Dwyer answered it. The call was from Miami, Florida, and the caller said he was "Moe," and he was looking for "Morris." When Dwyer said that Morris was in the kitchen having a sandwich, Moe quickly hung up. (Courtesy of the Brookline Police Department.)

Police believed that Harry "Doc" Sagansky was the brains behind a huge gambling syndicate and was a silent partner in some of the city's best-known nightclubs. Sagansky's criminal record went back to 1916. One of his earliest brushes with the law occurred in 1919, when he was fined $3 for "gaming on the Lord's Day." Sagansky was a spitfire until the very end. At the ripe old age of 90, he spent almost a year behind bars for refusing to testify before a grand jury. When he was finally released from the Plymouth County House of Correction in March 1989, he told a *Boston Globe* reporter: "It feels good to be out. I'm just going to go home and have some dinner." Sagansky lived to be 99 years old; he died in a Brookline nursing home in 1997. (Courtesy of the Brookline Police Department.)

Moe Weinstein (left) was a bookie from Revere who worked closely with Harry "Doc" Sagansky (below, right). Born on January 6, 1898, Sagansky worked as a newsboy in Boston's West End and went on to graduate from Tufts Dental School in 1918. He had a dental practice in Scollay Square, which may have been why he was called "Doc." Former Boston mayor James Michael Curley once got an $8,500 loan from Sagansky and, as security, Sagansky carried a $50,000 insurance policy on Curley's life. In 1965, Sagansky and Weinstein were sentenced to prison and fined $5,000 on charges of using interstate communication to register bets. (Both, courtesy of the Brookline Police Department.)

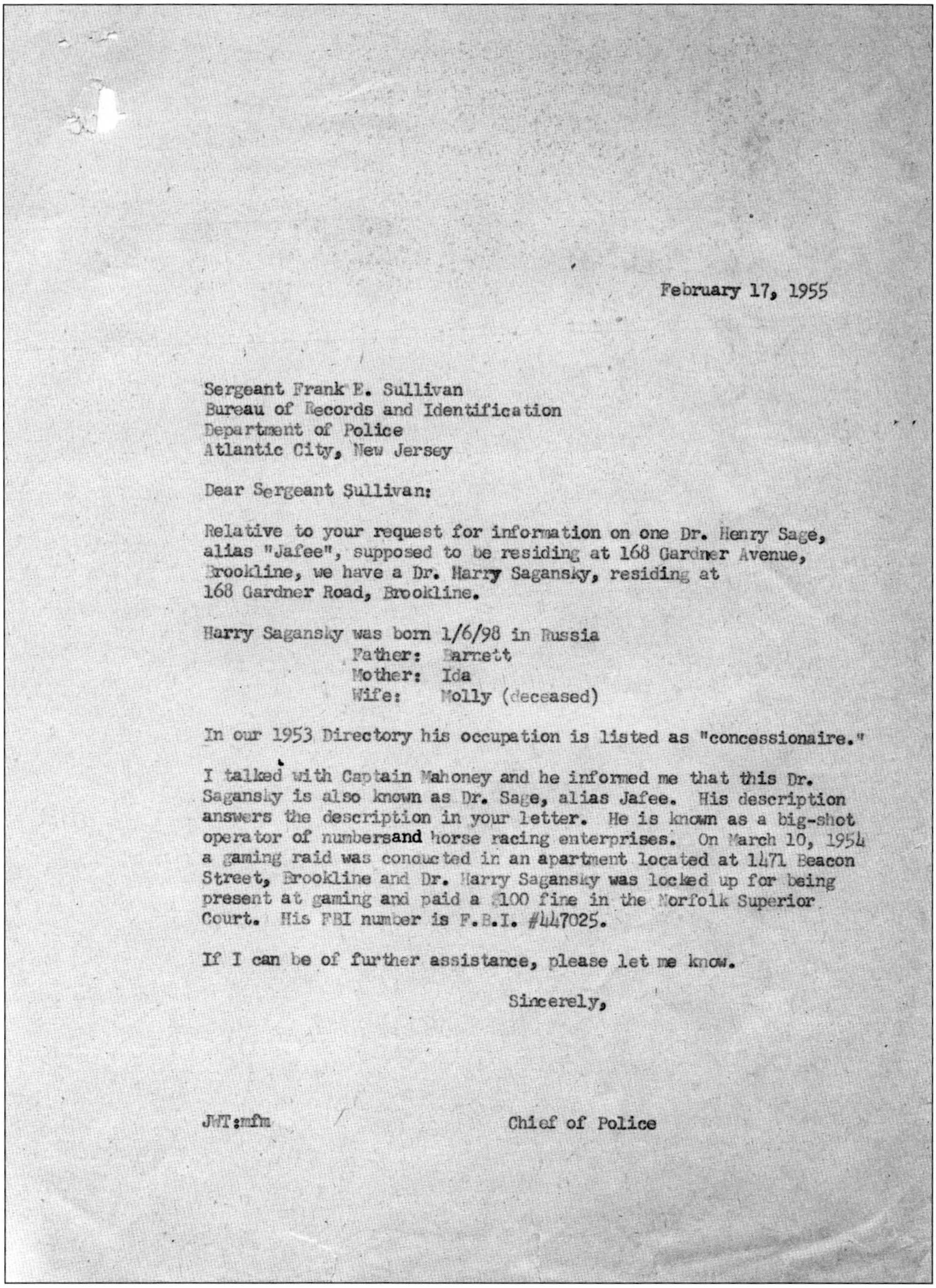

February 17, 1955

Sergeant Frank E. Sullivan
Bureau of Records and Identification
Department of Police
Atlantic City, New Jersey

Dear Sergeant Sullivan:

Relative to your request for information on one Dr. Henry Sage,
alias "Jafee", supposed to be residing at 168 Gardner Avenue,
Brookline, we have a Dr. Harry Sagansky, residing at
168 Gardner Road, Brookline.

Harry Sagansky was born 1/6/98 in Russia
                Father: Barnett
                Mother: Ida
                Wife: Molly (deceased)

In our 1953 Directory his occupation is listed as "concessionaire."

I talked with Captain Mahoney and he informed me that this Dr.
Sagansky is also known as Dr. Sage, alias Jafee. His description
answers the description in your letter. He is known as a big-shot
operator of numbers and horse racing enterprises. On March 10, 1954
a gaming raid was conducted in an apartment located at 1471 Beacon
Street, Brookline and Dr. Harry Sagansky was locked up for being
present at gaming and paid a $100 fine in the Norfolk Superior
Court. His FBI number is F.B.I. #447025.

If I can be of further assistance, please let me know.

                                    Sincerely,

JWT:mfm   Chief of Police

In 1955, police in Atlantic City, New Jersey, asked the Brookline Police Department for information about a man who fit the description of Harry "Doc" Sagansky. The Brookline police chief wrote back and said that Sagansky was known as "a big-shot operator of numbers and horse racing enterprises" who recently had to pay a $100 fine after the gambling raid at 1471 Beacon Street. (Courtesy of the Brookline Police Department.)

Joseph "Hoodsie" Hotze became known as a "numbers kingpin" in the 1930s and 1940s. On May 2, 1960, six police officers showed up on the doorstep of his home at 111 University Road in Brookline (above). They had obtained a search warrant because they believed Hotze had been actively taking bets from his house. Police rang the doorbell and announced that the gas company had arrived. His wife opened the door. Hotze told the officers he had stopped all of his gaming action two weeks ago. Police searched Hotze's car (left)—a 1958 Oldsmobile with Massachusetts plates registered to his wife—and found a brown leather Zenith radio case containing $4,010 in cash. Hotze was found guilty of promoting a lottery and registering bets on horse races. He was fined $4,000. (Both, courtesy of the Brookline Police Department.)

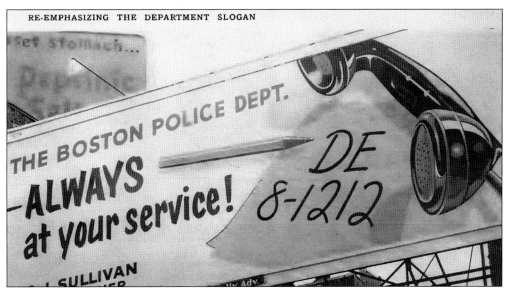

In the days before 911, people had to dial "DE 8-1212" to reach the Boston Police Department. This billboard, which was put up during Police Commissioner Leo J. Sullivan's tenure, shows the department slogan: "Always At Your Service!" (1960 Boston Police Commissioner's Annual Report.)

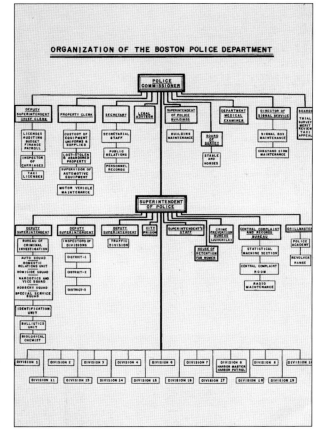

This is how the Boston Police Department was organized in 1960. The narcotics and vice squad investigated crimes against "chastity, morality, decency, and good order, involving the unlawful sale, distribution, and use of narcotic drugs and derivatives and the importing, printing, publishing, selling, distributing, or exhibiting of obscene or impure literature, prints, pictures"— activities that were the specialties of many organized crime syndicates. (1960 Boston Police Commissioner's Annual Report.)

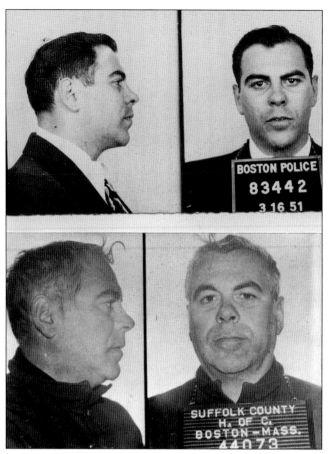

Joseph N. Palladino Jr. (also known as "Little Beans") was known to police as a pornography kingpin with connections to organized crime. He was born in June 1922 and lived in Saugus. In 1970, he was arrested and charged with distributing obscene literature. He said he worked as a "book distributor" at 694 Washington Street in downtown Boston. He was eventually convicted on pornography and tax evasion charges. (Both, courtesy of the Massachusetts State Police.)

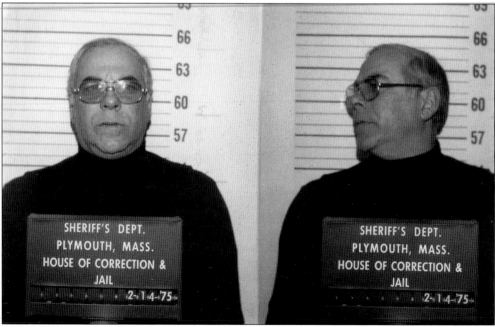

Four

THE RISE (AND FALL) OF THE MAFIA

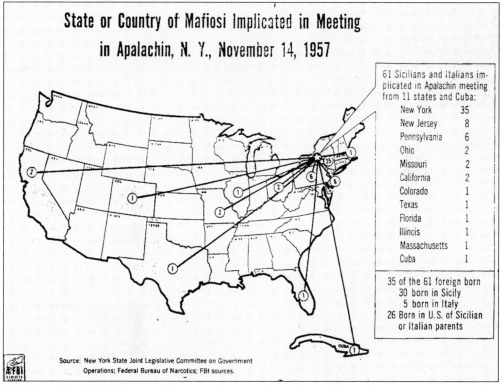

State or Country of Mafiosi Implicated in Meeting in Apalachin, N. Y., November 14, 1957

61 Sicilians and Italians implicated in Apalachin meeting from 11 states and Cuba:

New York	35
New Jersey	8
Pennsylvania	6
Ohio	2
Missouri	2
California	2
Colorado	1
Texas	1
Florida	1
Illinois	1
Massachusetts	1
Cuba	1

35 of the 61 foreign born
30 born in Sicily
5 born in Italy
26 Born in U.S. of Sicilian or Italian parents

Source: New York State Joint Legislative Committee on Government Operations; Federal Bureau of Narcotics; FBI sources.

On November 14, 1957, reputed organized crime figures from all over the country convened at the home of Joseph Barbara Sr. in Apalachin, New York. Sixty-one men came from 11 different states (one traveled from Cuba) to attend the meeting. The only attendee from Massachusetts was Frank Cucchiara. (Courtesy of the Federal Bureau of Investigation.)

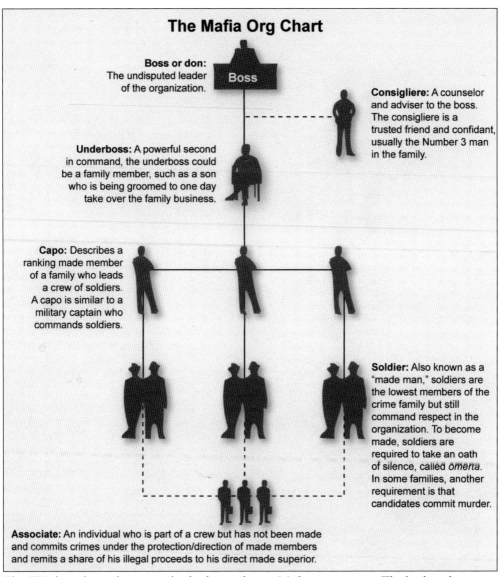

The Mafia Org Chart

Boss or don: The undisputed leader of the organization.

Boss

Consigliere: A counselor and adviser to the boss. The consigliere is a trusted friend and confidant, usually the Number 3 man in the family.

Underboss: A powerful second in command, the underboss could be a family member, such as a son who is being groomed to one day take over the family business.

Capo: Describes a ranking made member of a family who leads a crew of soldiers. A capo is similar to a military captain who commands soldiers.

Soldier: Also known as a "made man," soldiers are the lowest members of the crime family but still command respect in the organization. To become made, soldiers are required to take an oath of silence, called *omerta*. In some families, another requirement is that candidates commit murder.

Associate: An individual who is part of a crew but has not been made and commits crimes under the protection/direction of made members and remits a share of his illegal proceeds to his direct made superior.

This FBI chart shows the various leadership ranks in a Mafia organization. The leader is known as the "boss," the second in command is the "underboss," the adviser to the boss is the "consigliere," and a "capo" is a ranking made member who leads a crew of "soldiers." Members and associates are supposed to obey their superiors and get permission before engaging in criminal activity. The FBI authorities refer to the mob as La Cosa Nostra, which roughly translates to "this thing of ours" in Italian. (Courtesy of the Federal Bureau of Investigation.)

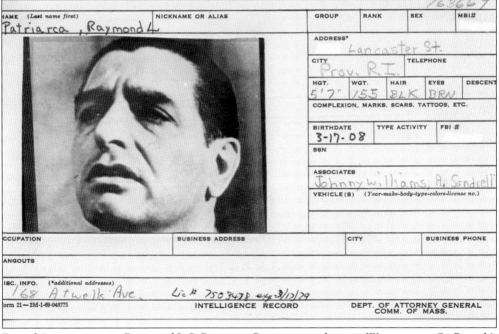

026247

NAME (Last name first)	NICKNAME OR ALIAS	GROUP	RANK	SEX	MBI#
BRUCCOLA, PHILIP	BUCCOLO; PHIL BUCALO FILIPO BUCCULA				

ADDRESS*		
CITY BOSTON		TELEPHONE

HGT. 5'6"	WGT. 160	HAIR GREY	EYES BRO	DESCEN ITAL

COMPLEXION, MARKS, SCARS, TATTOOS, ETC.

BIRTHDATE 7-8-86	TYPE ACTIVITY	FBI #

SSN

ASSOCIATES
ANTHONY SANDRELLI, JOHNNY WILLIAM

VEHICLE(S) (Year-make-body-type-colors-license no.)

OCCUPATION	BUSINESS ADDRESS	CITY	BUSINESS PHONE

HANGOUTS

Philip Bruccola (or Buccola) was one of Boston's earliest crime bosses. Born in Sicily in 1886, he immigrated to the United States in 1920 and then became head of the New England Mafia. He was known to pal around with Joe Lombardo, Anthony Sandrelli, and Johnny H. Williams and could often be seen at the Florentine Café in Boston's North End. He retired to Sicily in the 1950s. (Courtesy of the Massachusetts State Police.)

163667

NAME (Last name first)	NICKNAME OR ALIAS	GROUP	RANK	SEX	MBI#
Patriarca, Raymond L.					

ADDRESS* Lancaster St.		
CITY Prov. R.I.		TELEPHONE

HGT. 5'7"	WGT. 155	HAIR BLK	EYES BRN	DESCENT

COMPLEXION, MARKS, SCARS, TATTOOS, ETC.

BIRTHDATE 3-17-08	TYPE ACTIVITY	FBI #

SSN

ASSOCIATES
Johnny Williams, A. Sandrell

VEHICLE(S) (Year-make-body-type-colors-license no.)

OCCUPATION	BUSINESS ADDRESS	CITY	BUSINESS PHONE

HANGOUTS

MISC. INFO. (*additional addresses)		
168 Atwells Ave.	Lic # 750 3478 exp 3/17/29	

orm 21—2M-1-69-948775   INTELLIGENCE RECORD   DEPT. OF ATTORNEY GENERAL COMM. OF MASS.

Buccola's successor was Raymond L.S. Patriarca. Patriarca was born in Worcester on St. Patrick's Day (March 17), 1908, liked to smoke cigars, and was identified as "king of the rackets" in New England as early as 1950. Supt. John T. Howland, of the Boston police, told the *Boston Globe* that Patriarca "was looked upon with awe as a smooth, sure and careful man." (Courtesy of the Massachusetts State Police.)

DEPARTMENT OF POLICE, SPRINGFIELD, MASS. — DETECTIVE BUREAU

LEFT THUMB   RIGHT THUMB   PRISONER'S SIGNATURE

Raymond Patriarca

RESIDENCE *161 Atwells Ave, Providence R.I.*

ARRESTED BY *Lt Crowley Lt Kelliher Lt Fenton* DATE *12/9/37*

BERTILLON MEASUREMENTS

HEIGHT 1 M. 66.2	HD. LENGTH	R. EAR LENGTH	L. LIT. F.		BRIDGE	
STRETCH 1 M.	HD. WIDTH	L. FOOT	L. FOR. A.	NOSE	BASE	
TRUNK	CHEEK WIDTH	L. MID. F.	CHIN		DIMENSIONS	

BERTILLON MEASUREMENTS TAKEN BY *M. J. Collins* DATE *Dec. 9 1937*

AGE *29*
COLOR *white*
HEIGHT *5'5½"*
HAIR *Black*
WEIGHT *176*
COMPLEXION *Dark*
BUILD *stocky*
MUSTACHE

EYE *brown*
TEETH
BORDER
RIGHT EAR — LOBE
INCL.
FOREHEAD — HEIGHT
WIDTH

ALIASES
BORN *Worcester, Mass.*
CRIME *Vagrancy*

ALIASES
OCCUPATION *Mechanic*
DISPOSITION *Dec 11 1937 — Filed —*

Jewelry snatch thief and hold up man. classed as Public Enemy in Providence, R.I.
Turned over to Cambridge Mass. for larceny of auto.

In 1937, the Springfield Police Department described Raymond L. S. Patriarca as a 29-year-old "jewelry snatch thief and holdup man" who had been designated a "Public Enemy" in his adopted hometown of Providence, Rhode Island. He was listed as being five feet, five-and-a-half inches tall, with a weight of 176 pounds. Police photographed him in a pin-striped suit jacket, striped shirt, and striped tie. His black hair was slicked back, and his sleepy brown eyes stared solemnly at the camera. (Courtesy of the Massachusetts State Police.)

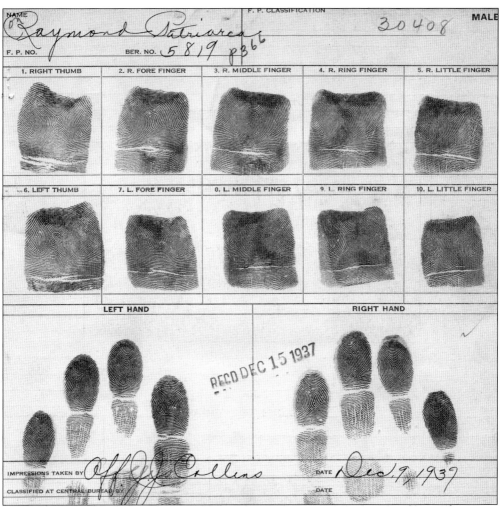

The Springfield police also fingerprinted Patriarca in 1937. Soon after, he was convicted and sentenced to three to five years in prison on charges of carrying a gun without a permit, possession of burglar's tools, and robbing a Brookline jewelry business. (Courtesy of the Massachusetts State Police.)

On March 6, 1962, the FBI installed secret microphones at Raymond L.S. Patriarca's office at the Coin-O-Matic Distributors and National Cigarette Service, his vending machine and pinball game business, located at 168 Atwells Avenue in Providence, Rhode Island. His office was bugged until July 12, 1965. (Courtesy of the Massachusetts State Police.)

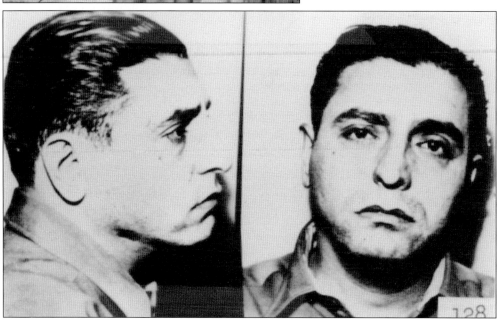

Three months into the FBI's surveillance operation, the special agent in charge in Boston sent a memo to FBI director J. Edgar Hoover informing him that the microphone surveillance at Patriarca's office "has shown that Patriarca exerts real control over the racketeers and racketeering activities in Rhode Island and Massachusetts." (Courtesy of the Federal Bureau of Investigation.)

Joseph Lombardo (above) was not happy when he and his old comrades, like Henry Selvitella (alias Noyes), were accused of being part of La Cosa Nostra at a US Senate committee hearing in 1963. Lombardo told a *Boston Globe* sportswriter that he and his friends were older and wiser; their wild days were long over. "That was 40 years ago, and now it's made to look like something new. Old stories, 40 years old. Henry Noyes is supposed to be a tough man. Henry is old and sick and if he stays up past nine o'clock, that's a big deal for him." (Courtesy of the Massachusetts State Police.)

Ilario M.A. Zannino was also known by his alias, Larry Baione. He lived at 213 Harrison Avenue in the South End. In the early hours of March 6, 1951, 30-year-old Zannino got into a shoot-out with 28-year-old James Bratsos. Prosecutors said Zannino showed up at Bratsos's home on Davis Street after they had gotten into an argument at a local bar. Zannino was injured in the gun battle and later recovered under guard at Boston City Hospital. (Courtesy of the Massachusetts State Police.)

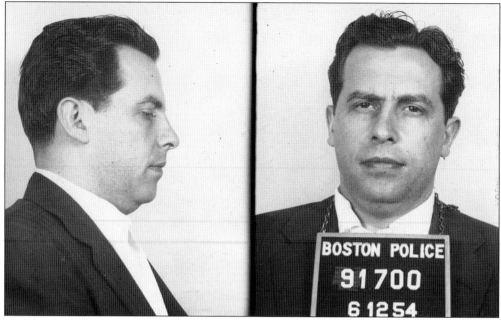

In the spring of 1954, James Bratsos (the archrival of Zannino, pictured above) disappeared. Bratsos had just been released from prison after serving a two-and-a-half-year sentence for breaking and entering. On December 5, 1954, Boston police received a tip that the 31-year-old ex-con's body might be in Stoughton: "Do you know where Glen Echo Lake is?" said the mysterious caller. "Look in the bottom and you'll find Bratsos." He was never found. (Courtesy of the Massachusetts State Police.)

In the book *Hitman: The Untold Story of Johnny Martorano*, Howie Carr writes that Baione had killed Bratsos and disposed of his body. Zannino moved to Moraine Street in Jamaica Plain and then to the suburban town of Swampscott. He was known to pal around with Anthony Santaniello, Henry Selvitella, Frank Cucchiara, Raymond L.S. Patriarca, and Joe Lombardo. Zannino was indicted on racketeering charges in 1983 and died in federal prison in March 1996. He was 75 years old. (Courtesy of the Massachusetts State Police.)

Although he was short in stature (five feet, three-and-a-half inches), Frank Cucchiara became a big name in the North End. A native Sicilian, he owned the Purity Cheese Co. on Endicott Street and was known to frequent Giro's, a restaurant on Hanover Street. One of his early brushes with the law occurred in 1925, when he was arrested for possession of morphine and dynamite. He was also held as a suspect in the 1931 murder of Gustin Gang leader Frank Wallace and Barney "Dodo" Walsh. Years later, Cucchiara was accused of being the Massachusetts delegate at the infamous 1957 "underworld summit" in Apalachin, New York. He was later acquitted on lack of evidence. (Courtesy of the FBI.)

John H. "Johnny" Williams (also known as John Guglielmo and Chick Williams) was a longtime La Cosa Nostra member from Revere who became a key player in Boston's underworld scene during the 1940s and 1950s. Boston police knew him as the right-hand man of Phil Buccola. (Courtesy of the Massachusetts State Police.)

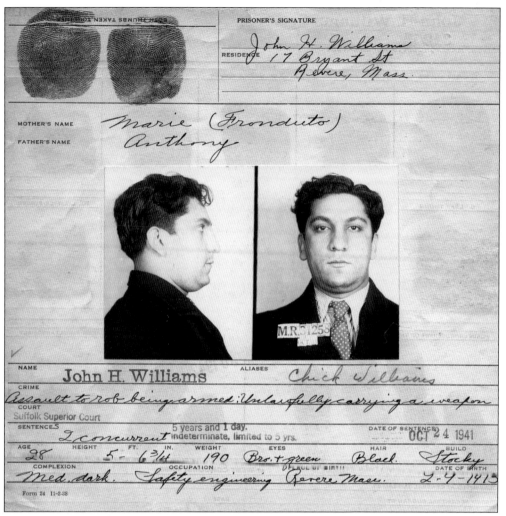

In October 1941, Williams was sentenced in Suffolk Superior Court on charges of armed robbery and unlawfully carrying a weapon. He was 28 years old at the time, a stocky guy who weighed 190 pounds and stood less than five feet, seven inches tall. Authorities described him as having brown and green eyes and an interesting job title: "safety engineering." (Courtesy of the Massachusetts State Police.)

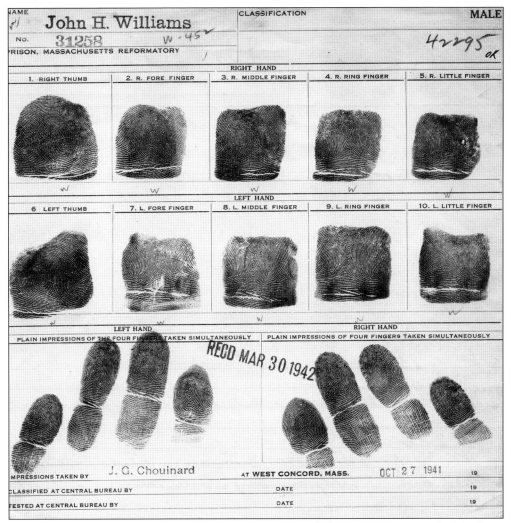

Williams was sentenced to five years in prison. He was paroled in 1944 to serve in the Merchant Marines. Later, in the 1950s, Williams went to Cuba and reportedly got involved with The Tropicana, one of the biggest and most famous nightclubs of the time. (Courtesy of the Massachusetts State Police.)

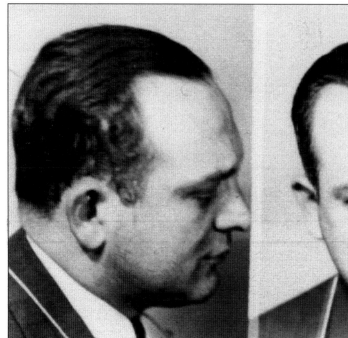

Anthony Santaniello looks like a Hollywood movie star in this undated FBI photograph. Born in 1903, Santaniello was known as "the old man" and "the arbitrator" of the New England Mafia. Authorities pegged him as a shylock and a bookie. He lived in Brookline, operated the Paddock Bar at 255 Tremont Street, and was known to frequent Giro's in the North End. (Courtesy of the Federal Bureau of Investigation.)

Anthony Sandrelli lived on Prince Street in Boston's North End. He was born in Canada, which earned him the nickname "Tony Canadian." This photograph was taken in 1949, when he was 41 years old. His shoes are shiny, his pinstriped pants are perfectly pressed, and his fedora hat is cocked slightly to one side. Notice the ring on his pinky finger. According to police, Sandrelli operated an after-hours club. (Courtesy of the Brookline Police Department.)

Joseph Anselmo (also known as Joe Burns) was a reputed organized crime figure who hung out with Anthony Sandrelli and Romeo Martin. He was allegedly involved in bookmaking, and his criminal record included arrests for breaking and entering, carrying a concealed weapon, and receiving stolen goods. He previously lived in Somerset, Somerville, and Arlington. (Courtesy of the Massachusetts State Police.)

Michael Rocco (also known as Mickey the Wiseguy) stood five feet, three inches tall and had grey-blue eyes. He lived in Boston, East Boston, and Revere. His record went back to 1916, and he had been arrested dozens of times. In 1966, he allegedly slapped an IRS agent at Logan Airport, which resulted in another arrest. He received a suspended jail sentence, three years of probation, and a $3,000 fine. (Courtesy of the Federal Bureau of Investigation.)

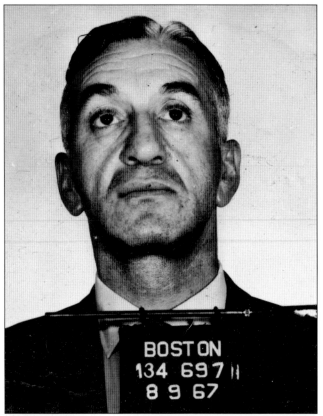

Mafia underboss Gennaro J. "Jerry" Angiulo rose to power in Boston during the 1960s. He was described by FBI director J. Edgar Hoover as a veteran member of La Cosa Nostra, "over-all boss of rackets in the Boston area," and "chief lieutenant of Raymond L.S. Patriarca, notorious New England hoodlum." In 1963, the FBI bugged his club, Jay's Lounge, located at 255 Tremont Street in Boston. (Courtesy of the Massachusetts State Police.)

On September 19, 1983, FBI agents arrested Jerry Angiulo at Francesco's restaurant in Boston's North End. As the feds led him out the door in handcuffs, he yelled, "I'll be back before my pork chops get cold." Angiulo ended up serving 24 years in prison. He was released in 2007 and died a free man two years later, at the age of 90. (Courtesy of the Massachusetts State Police.)

Gennaro "Jerry" Angiulo's office was located at 98 Prince Street in the North End. Law enforcement officials accused Angiulo and his cohorts of racketeering, gambling, and loan-sharking, and they identified Angiulo as the underboss of the organization. This is what 98 Prince Street looks like today. (Photograph by Emily Sweeney.)

This undated surveillance photograph shows Samuel S. Granito (left) walking, with newspaper in hand, alongside Fred Simone. Law enforcement officials said Granito was a "capo regime" (captain) in the New England mob and was friends with Brink's robbery suspect Anthony Pino. In 1986, Granito was sentenced in a racketeering case, along with the Angiulo brothers, to 20 years and slapped with a $35,000 fine. (Courtesy of the Massachusetts State Police.)

Ralph Lamattina is smoking a cigarette while chatting with a friend in this undated surveillance photograph. Born in July 1922, Lamattina was well known in Boston's North End, where he ran the Nite Lite Café. His nickname was "Ching Chong;" he was also known in the streets as "Ralphie Chong." (Courtesy of the Massachusetts State Police.)

This is an undated surveillance photograph of Larry Zannino. Law enforcement officials believed that Zannino, Gennaro "Jerry" Angiulo, Samuel Granito, and Ralph Lamattina were making money from gambling operations in Boston's North End. (Courtesy of the Massachusetts State Police.)

High-stakes poker games were once played here, at 51 North Margin Street in the North End. Electronic surveillance was also conducted here from January to May 1981. FBI agents monitored members of the Patriarca family of La Cosa Nostra as they came and went from this building and 98 Prince Street. Today, 51 North Margin Street is home to a pet grooming business called The Dogfather. (Photograph by Emily Sweeney.)

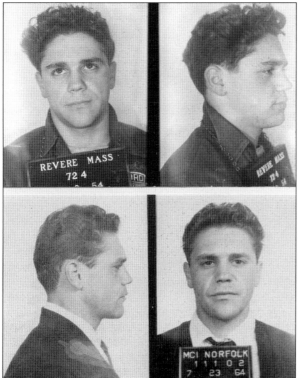

Mafia soldier Angelo "Sonny" Mercurio helped the FBI get the first-ever recording of a mob induction ceremony in October 1989. Mercurio later entered the federal witness protection program. He died in April 2007 in Little Rock, Arkansas, at the age of 70. (Courtesy of the Massachusetts State Police.)

The Mafia initiation ceremony took place on October 29, 1989, inside this modest single-family home at 34 Guild Street in Medford. Four members were "made" and pledged their lives to La Cosa Nostra at the ceremony, which was attended by Raymond Patriarca Jr., Joseph "J.R." Russo, and other reputed mobsters. The *Boston Globe* reported that each of the inductees took an oath, had their trigger finger pricked to draw blood, and burned a holy card—featuring a picture of the patron saint of the Patriarca family—in their cupped hands. This was the first time law enforcement had recorded a secret Mafia ritual of this kind. "Only the f---in' ghost knows what really took place over here, today, by God," said one La Cosa Nostra member during the induction ceremony. But little did they know, the FBI was listening. (Photograph by Emily Sweeney.)

Five

WINTER HILL VS. THE McLAUGHLINS

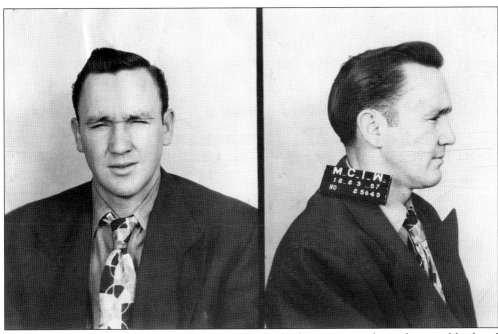

George P. McLaughlin and his brothers came from Charlestown, a working-class neighborhood in Boston that is home to the Bunker Hill monument. This photograph was taken in 1957, when McLaughlin was 30 years old. He was not a big guy—according to jail records, he stood five feet, five inches tall and only weighed 123 pounds. Once upon a time, the McLaughlin brothers were pals with a bunch of guys from the Winter Hill section of Somerville. But that friendship turned ugly. (Courtesy of the Brookline Police Department.)

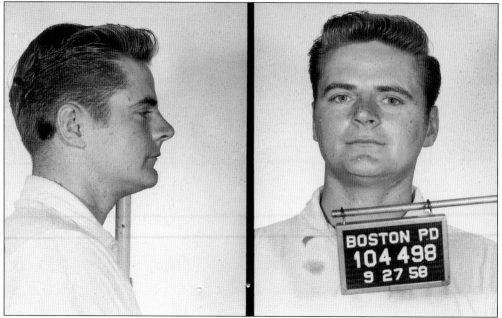

James J. McLean (above) was a charismatic kid who hailed from the Winter Hill section of Somerville, the urban, working class city next door to Charlestown. He was tough and handsome, and people gravitated to him. McLean and his associates battled the McLaughlin brothers for years. The feud supposedly started over a fight that took place in a cottage in Salisbury Beach when Georgie McLaughlin tried to grope the wife of McLean's friend. The McLean crew beat Georgie so badly that he had to be hospitalized. According to the FBI, many of the gangland murders in Greater Boston during the 1960s were the result of bad blood between the McLaughlins and the boys from Winter Hill. (Courtesy of the Massachusetts State Police.)

Howard T. "Howie" Winter (left) was a friend of Buddy McLean and Alexander F. Petricone. According to a *Boston Globe* article, on December 19, 1959, Winter and Petricone were among 25 people arrested in Somerville when state troopers conducted a gambling sting at drinking establishments around the city. At the time, district attorney John J. Droney declared: "This is the beginning of an all-out war on gambling in Middlesex County." (Courtesy of the Massachusetts State Police.)

On September 4, 1962, Alexander F. Petricone's wife, Grace, borrowed Howie Winter's car to drive to a nearby bakery, and a hidden bomb attached to the car detonated while she was behind the wheel. Police believed the car bomb was intended for Winter. Luckily, she was not hurt. (Courtesy of the Massachusetts State Police.)

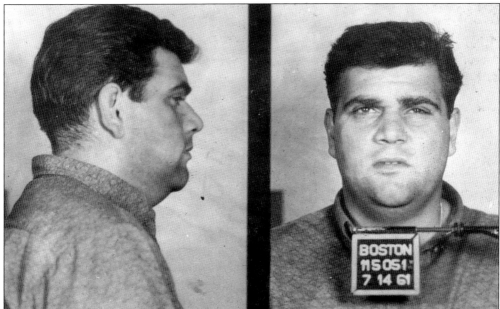

When the gang wars started heating up, McLean urged Petricone (above) to get out of town. He ended up moving to the West Coast, where he began his career as a Hollywood actor. Using the stage name Alex Rocco, he appeared in several television shows and movies, including the 1973 movie *The Friends of Eddie Coyle* and the 1972 mobster film *The Godfather,* in which he recites one of the movie's most memorable lines: "Do you know who I am? I'm Moe Greene!" (Courtesy of the Massachusetts State Police.)

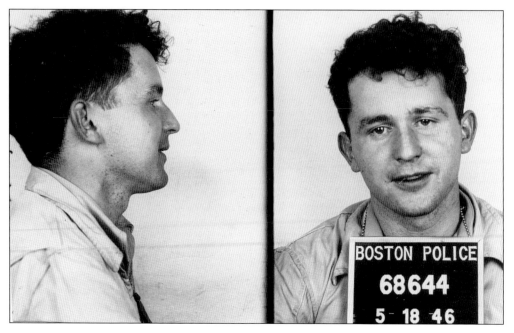

Bernard J. "Bernie" McLaughlin and his brothers were notorious in their neighborhood of Charlestown and the neighboring community of Somerville. One day in October 1961, someone wired dynamite underneath Buddy McLean's car in Somerville; the McLaughlins were the obvious suspects. A few days later, on October 31, 1961, Bernie McLaughlin was gunned down in broad daylight at noon in City Square, Charlestown. He was 40 years old. (Both, courtesy of the Massachusetts State Police.)

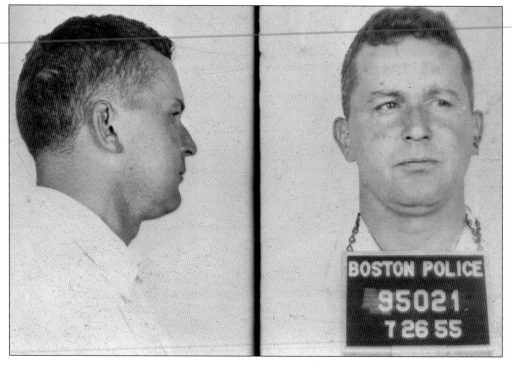

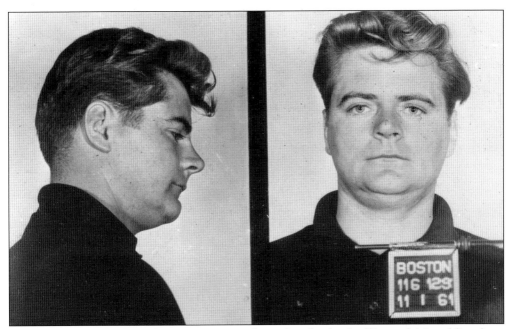

Buddy McLean and Alexander Petricone were charged in the death of Bernie McLaughlin after a witness identified McLean as the shooter and Petricone as the getaway driver. In December 1961, a Suffolk County grand jury cleared them of the charges. This photograph shows James J. "Buddy" McLean after he was picked up as a suspect in McLaughlin's murder. At the time, McLean was five feet, nine inches tall and weighed 170 pounds. He had blue eyes, light brown hair, and lived at 20 Radcliffe Road in Somerville. (Courtesy of the Massachusetts State Police.)

McLean was gunned down on Broadway, in the Winter Hill section of Somerville, on October 30, 1965. He had just left a Winter Hill barroom with Anthony D'Agostino, of East Boston, and Americo Sacramone, of Everett. Before leaving, McLean approached the detail officer on duty at the lounge, Edward Kelly, and playfully shined his badge, saying, "That's for luck." (Courtesy of the Massachusetts State Police.)

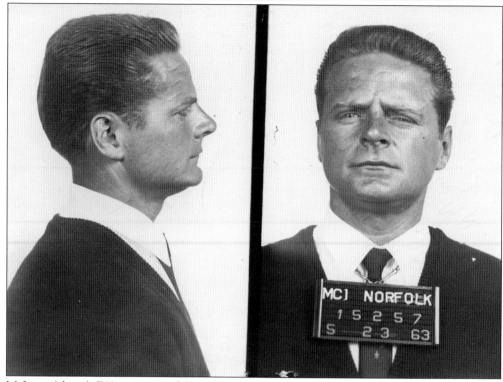

McLean (above), D'Agostino, and Sacramone were walking across Broadway to get to their cars when a gunman suddenly opened fire. McLean had a .38-caliber pistol tucked into his belt and over $1,000 in cash in his pockets. McLean's two companions survived the shooting—Sacramone suffered minor scalp wounds and D'Agostino's left arm was shattered. (Courtesy of the Massachusetts State Police.)

On January 7, 1965, the Boston FBI office sent a memo to FBI director J. Edgar Hoover (left) informing him that "Patriarca had told the group [on January 4, 1965] that is too bad the McLeans and the McLaughlins could not settle their feud over a handshake[.]" The assassination of Buddy McLean did not stop the killings. Gang warfare, fueled by the McLean-McLaughlin feud, would persist in the Boston area, and the body count would continue to rise. (Courtesy of the Federal Bureau of Investigation.)

On the night of March 14, 1964, George P. McLaughlin was hanging out at 55 Yeoman Street in Roxbury when he got into an argument with someone attending a party in the second-floor apartment. The skirmish ended with McLaughlin shooting 21-year-old William J. Sheridan in the head. (Courtesy of the Massachusetts State Police.)

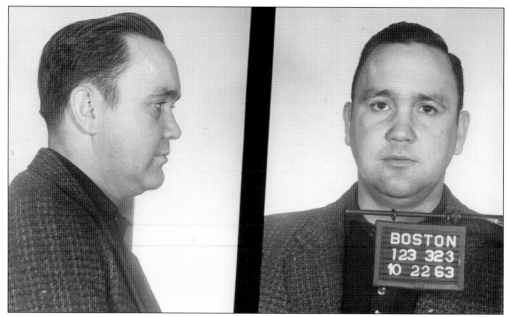

George P. McLaughlin, who was known to police for his lengthy criminal record, had previously been convicted of larceny, breaking and entering, assault to murder, and carrying a gun illegally. After shooting Sheridan, McLaughlin went on the lam. (Courtesy of the Massachusetts State Police.)

George P. McLaughlin was added to the FBI's 10 Most Wanted list in May 1964. The FBI poster said that McLaughlin, who was 36 years old, was "noted for a mean and nasty disposition, is reportedly extremely vicious when intoxicated and has been described as a 'nut' who would shoot his best friend if his back was turned." The poster noted that McLaughlin received a bad-conduct discharge from the US Navy and was known to have "a psychopathic personality" and "aggressive tendencies." (Courtesy of the Brookline Police Department.)

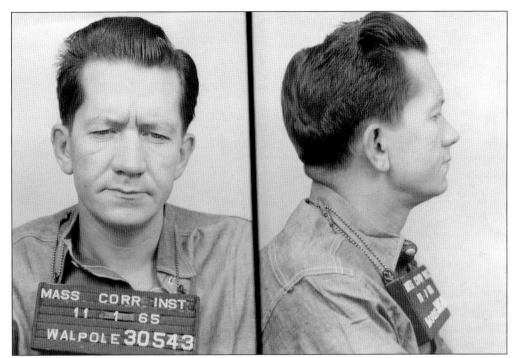

On February 24, 1965, FBI agents found George McLaughlin with his pal, James "Spike" O'Toole (pictured), in a third-story bedroom at 24 Duke Street in Mattapan. McLaughlin was half-dressed, and police found three revolvers tucked away in the top drawer of a dresser in the bedroom. O'Toole was sentenced to five to six years in state prison for helping out McLaughlin while he was on the lam. McLaughlin was convicted and sentenced to die. (Courtesy of the Massachusetts Department of Correction.)

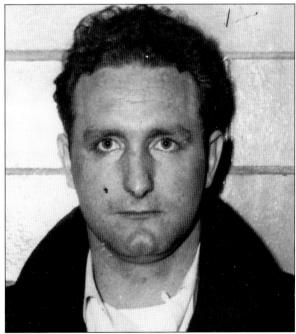

Born on March 17, 1929, Howie Winter was a tough guy and reputed gang leader from Somerville. "No one you'd want to take on alone," according to police sources. The first reference to the so-called "Winter Hill Gang" in the Boston Globe appeared in 1978, when Anthony Paul Ciulla took the stand and testified that Howie Winter, James J. "Whitey" Bulger, the Martorano brothers, Stevie Flemmi, and Joe McDonald were involved in fixing horse races. Winter and several other members of the so-called Winter Hill Gang were indicted by a grand jury for racketeering and scheming to fix races and bribe jockeys at racetracks in New England. Winter went to jail and was released in 2002. (Courtesy of the Massachusetts State Police.)

This garage at 12 Marshall Street was once owned by Howie Winter and reportedly served as the headquarters for the Winter Hill Gang. In 2008, Winter sold the garage to a Pentecostal church for $330,000. Today, the beige-colored stucco building is used as a house of worship and is home to the Greater Works Church of God Somerville. (Photograph by Emily Sweeney.)

Six

GANG WARS

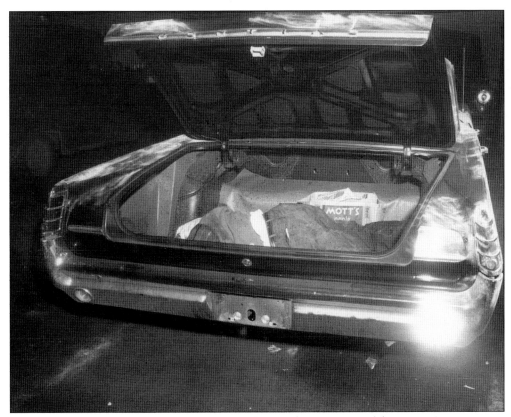

Francis R. Benjamin, 32, was one of many casualties in the gang wars of the 1960s. An ex-convict and father of six, he had just been released from Walpole State Prison, where he was doing time for armed robbery, when he was killed in May 1964. His decapitated body was found in the trunk of this car in South Boston's Old Harbor Village, a housing project that was renamed after Mary Ellen McCormack. His head was never found. (Courtesy of the Massachusetts State Police.)

Harold R. Hannon (above) was another victim of the gang wars of the 1960s. He was 54 years old, lived in Everett, and had a lengthy criminal record that went back 40 years and included charges of larceny, burglary, and drugs. He was friends with the McLaughlin brothers and Edward "Teddy" Deegan, a local burglar who also met an untimely death. (Above, courtesy of the Massachusetts State Police; below, courtesy of the Brookline Police Department.)

```
13393   FILE 19   SP BOSTON MASS   OCT 16-63
TO      SP FRAMINGHAM   CCC   A-7

DEFENDANT      EDWARD C. DEEGAN   DOB 1-2-30
ADDRESS        52 ASHTON ST EVERETT, MASS.
CHARGE         SP B& E NT WITH INTENT COMMIT FELONY 266-14
OFFICERS       S/SGT JJ KULIK & TPR JR O,DONOVAN SSU & INSP H. DOHERTY,
                                                      PD EVERETT


          ON 10-16-63 AT APPROX 9-00 PM AS RESULT OF INVEST &
INFO RECEIVED -- OFFICERS LOCATED AND APPHD ABOVE SUBJECT/DEFENDANT/
OPERATING MV ON FERRY ST EVERETT. DEFENDANT WANTED BY PD BROOKLINE IN
CONNECTION WITH BE&L DWELLING HOUSE ON OCT 4TH 1963. /REFER TO
PD BROOKLINE IT 700 FILE 5 GA DATED 10-5-63 RE ABOVE DEFENDANT AND
ONE GEORGE P. MCLAUGHLIN WANTED FOR BE - NT / ALSO / PD BROOKLINE
IT 701 FILE 13 IO GA DATED 10-5-63 RE A CO-DEFENDANT ONE HAROLD R. HANNON
INVOLVED SAME CASE./

          DEFENDANT TURNED OVER TO LIEUT JC ROURKE PD BROOKLINE -
INVEST DEFENDANT.

AUTH CAPT JR MORIARTY    SOUZA   10-55 PM
END
```

Hannon turned up dead in August 1964, when his nude body washed ashore near Logan Airport. He had been blindfolded, bound and gagged, and tied with rope and tape in what authorities described as a "Chinese strangle knot." (Courtesy of the Massachusetts State Police.)

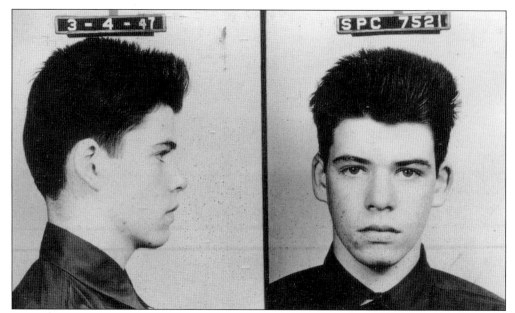

Ronald P. Dermody was a hazel-eyed boy with brown curly hair and a knack for getting into trouble. When this photograph was taken, he was just a teenager who stood five feet, seven inches tall and weighed 120 pounds. His listed address was 54 Webster Avenue in Cambridge. One of his earliest run-ins with the law took place on April 24, 1946, when he was charged with being a delinquent child. (Courtesy of the Massachusetts State Police.)

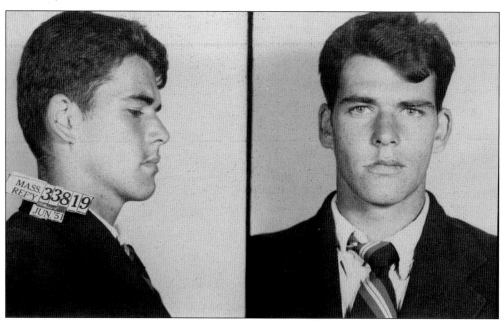

Dermody got into deeper trouble with the law in 1956, when he was convicted of robbing a bank with James J. "Whitey" Bulger. He ended up serving eight years in prison. (Courtesy of the Massachusetts State Police.)

Dermody was 25 years old when he was sentenced for the bank robbery. None of the stolen money was recovered. Dermody told probation officers that he used his share of the loot—$14,000—to pay for his wedding. (Courtesy of the Massachusetts State Police.)

MASSACHUSETTS DEPARTMENT OF PUBLIC SAFETY, BUREAU OF IDENTIFICATION

Name **DERMODY   RONALD   P.**
(Type or Print)   Last   First   Middle

Record from .... **Mass. State Police**

No. .... Previous No. ....

NOTE IN SPACE BELOW REASON FOR MISSING OR POOR IMPRESSIONS DUE TO AMPUTATIONS, DEFORMITY, INJURY OR CONDITION OF HANDS

1. Right Thumb	2. Right Index Finger	3. Right Middle Finger	4. Right Ring Finger	5. Right Little Finger

6. Left Thumb	7. Left Index Finger	8. Left Middle Finger	9. Left Ring Finger	10. Left Little Finger

Impressions taken by: (Signature) *Arthur W. Morison 190*   Department (if different) and Title **Trooper**   Date **9-5-64**

Four fingers taken simultaneously	Left Thumb	Right Thumb	Four fingers taken simultaneously
LEFT			RIGHT

The victim was shot and killed on 9-4-64 in Watertown. He was later
fingerprinted at the Watson Funeral Home, 11 Magazine Street
Cambridge. Fingerprinted on 9-5-64.

Dermody was murdered on September 4, 1964. Authorities took these fingerprints the day after he died. (Courtesy of the Massachusetts State Police.)

Dermody's body was found inside his car, which was parked at the corner of Belmont and School Streets in Watertown. He had been shot three times in the head. (Courtesy of the Massachusetts State Police.)

A pair of eyeglasses and pack of cigarettes sit on the bloodstained front seats of Dermody's car. (Courtesy of the Massachusetts State Police.)

George E. Ash was murdered in late December 1964. The outlaw brother of a Boston police officer, he went to reform school as a kid and did time in state prison for armed robbery. He had just been released from prison when he was killed. His body was found in this sedan, parked across the street from St. Philip's Church on Harrison Avenue in Boston's South End. Ash was hunched over in the passenger seat with his coat pulled over his head. He had been stabbed in the back more than 50 times. (Courtesy of the Massachusetts State Police.)

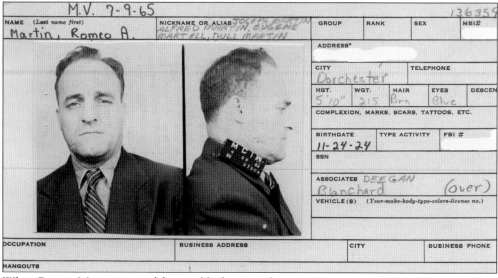

When Romeo Martin escaped from jail by hitting a home run in a prison baseball game in 1951, newspapers called him "The Home Run Hood." He had been playing in a prison all-star game at Washington State Penitentiary when he hit a ball far into the woods. He ran to first base and then . . . just kept running. He was eventually caught in his hometown of Boston, six months later. Martin was a convicted burglar who enjoyed writing poetry and was known to quote Emerson. In July 1965, he was shot and killed by Joseph "The Animal" Barboza. His body, found in Revere, was in the front seat of his red convertible with the motor still running. He had been shot five times in the chest. (Courtesy of the Massachusetts State Police.)

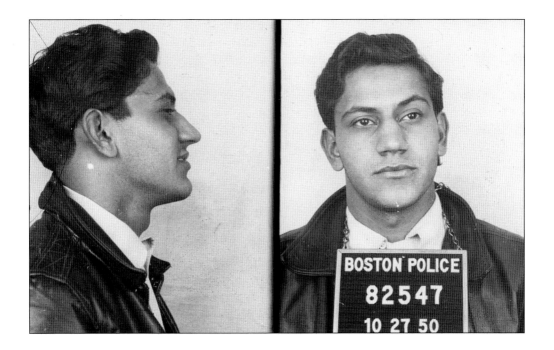

Arthur "Tash" Bratsos was the younger brother of James Bratsos, who disappeared in 1954. Like his older brother, he met an untimely death. He was shot and killed at the Nite Lite Café on Commercial Street in November 1966. Police said Bratsos had been arrested a few weeks before with Joseph "The Animal" Barboza and had been trying to raise bail money for Barboza so he could get out of jail. (Both, courtesy of the Massachusetts State Police.)

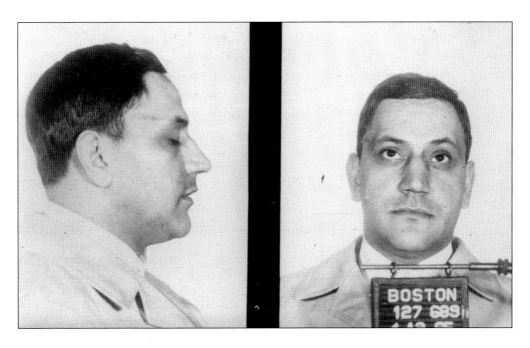

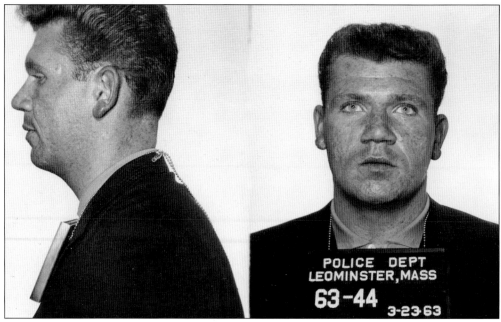

Thomas DePrisco was a burly redhead from Roslindale. He was 24 years old when he was murdered, along with Arthur Bratsos, at the Nite Lite Café in November 1966. DePrisco and Bratsos were found in the backseat of Bratsos's gray Cadillac, which was parked at the corner of A and West Fourth Streets in South Boston. Blood was all over the inside of the car. The Associated Press reported that they were the 34th and 35th victims in the two-and-half-year underworld gang war. The manager of the Nite Lite, "Ralphie Chong" Lamattina, later pleaded guilty to charges of being an accessory after the fact of murder in connection with the case, but he would not say who pulled the trigger. (Both, courtesy of the Massachusetts State Police.)

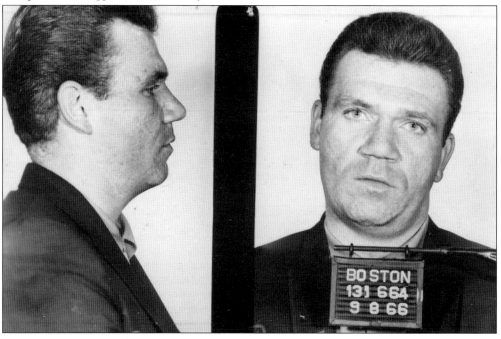

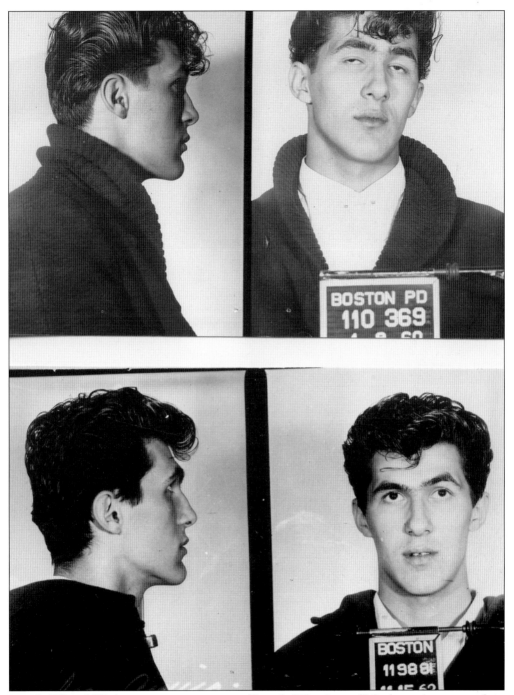

Joseph "Chico" W. Amico was an associate of Joseph "The Animal" Barboza. Amico stood six feet tall and had brown eyes, thick eyebrows and dark wavy hair. He was 24 years old when he was shot to death in Revere in December 1966. At the time of his murder, his pal Barboza was locked up in the Charles Street Jail. The Associated Press reported that it was the 36th gangland slaying in Greater Boston in two and a half years. (Courtesy of the Massachusetts State Police.)

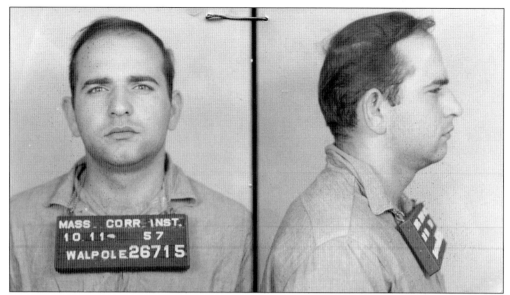

Vincent J. "Jimmy the Bear" Flemmi was a violent thug who was suspected of murdering Edward "Teddy" Deegan, Frank Benjamin, and other local hoods during the Irish Gang Wars of the 1960s. He also once served as an informant for the FBI. In 1957, he was sent to prison for robbing the Boston & Albany Railroad Employees Credit Union in South Station. (Courtesy of the Massachusetts Department of Correction.)

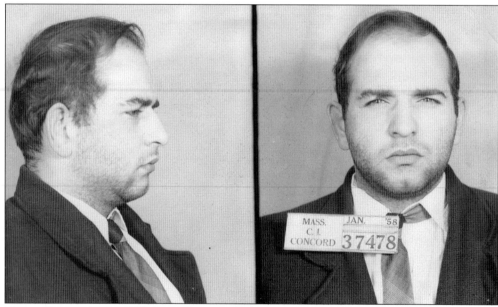

Here is "Jimmy the Bear" Flemmi, photographed in a suit and tie in January 1958. Flemmi was a tough guy. In September 1964, he was shot six times by two gunmen on Bird Street in Dorchester and managed to survive. He got shot again in May 1965, when he was ambushed outside his home at 699 Adams Street in Dorchester. In the second shooting, the two men left him for dead on the sidewalk, but once again, he lived to tell the tale . . . just not to the police. Police Commissioner Edmund McNamara said investigators questioned Flemmi at the hospital, but he would not say who was after him. (Courtesy of the Massachusetts Department of Correction.)

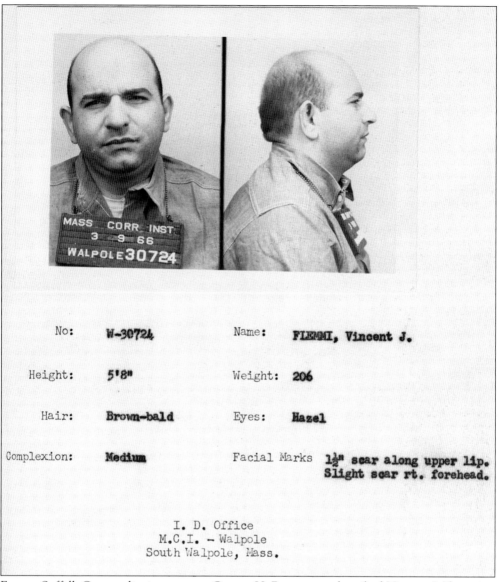

No:	W-30724	Name:	FLEMMI, Vincent J.
Height:	5'8"	Weight:	206
Hair:	Brown-bald	Eyes:	Hazel
Complexion:	Medium	Facial Marks	1½" scar along upper lip. Slight scar rt. forehead.

I. D. Office
M.C.I. — Walpole
South Walpole, Mass.

Former Suffolk County district attorney Garrett H. Byrne once described Vincent J. Flemmi as "a vicious individual with a record a mile long." Even behind bars, Flemmi had enemies. In 1968, Flemmi was stabbed in prison and had to be hospitalized. After Flemmi survived that attack, one police desk clerk said: "He's got more lives than a cat." (Courtesy of the Massachusetts Department of Correction.)

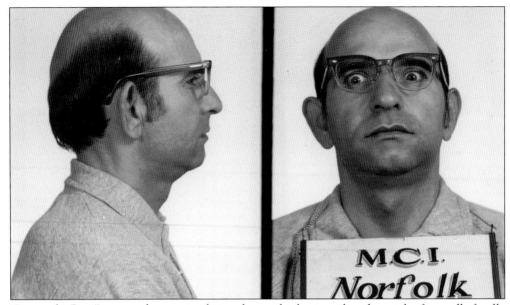

"Jimmy the Bear" managed to survive being shot multiple times, but the prick of a needle finally did him in. Flemmi sported horn-rimmed eyeglasses—and a crazy-looking facial expression—when this photograph was taken in June 1979, while he was doing time at MCI-Norfolk. A few months later, on October 16, 1979, Flemmi died from a drug overdose while in prison. (Courtesy of the Massachusetts Department of Correction.)

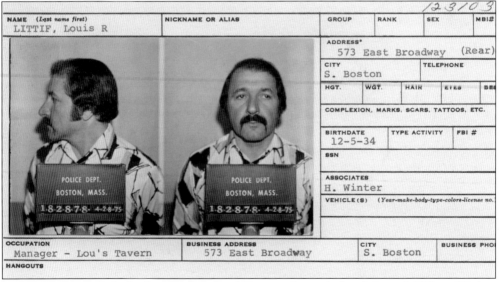

Louis R. Litif was a flashy bookmaker from South Boston who worked with James J. "Whitey" Bulger and Stephen J. "The Rifleman" Flemmi. According to a lawsuit filed by Litif's widow, after Litif was indicted on murder charges in 1979, he considered cooperating with authorities by snitching on Bulger and Flemmi. Litif was killed before he could make a deal with law enforcement. Court documents state that Litif was last seen alive in April 1980 at Triple O's in South Boston, where he was assaulted by Bulger and an associate and stabbed dozens of times with a sharp object and then shot in the neck. His body was later discovered stuffed inside a green garbage bag in the trunk of his car in the South End. (Courtesy of the Massachusetts State Police.)

Richard J. Castucci owned the Ebb Tide Lounge, a Revere nightclub that was popular hangout for underworld hoods. In December 1976, Castucci was found dead in the trunk of his wife's Cadillac. He was wrapped in a blue sleeping bag, dead from a single gunshot wound to his right temple. Police believed the killer was someone Castucci knew because the shot was fired at such a close range. (Both, courtesy of the Massachusetts State Police.)

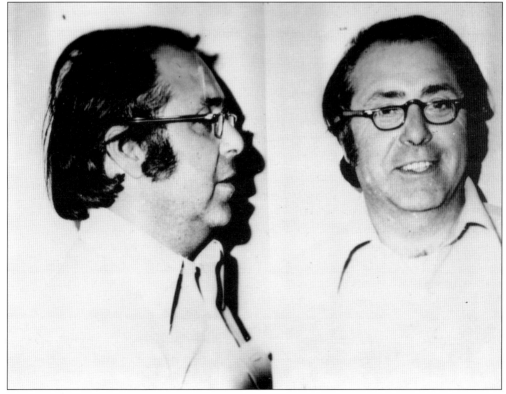

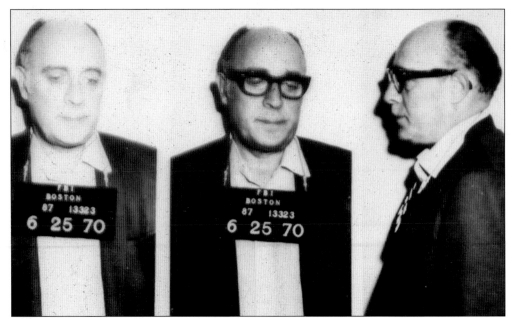

Phil Waggenheim was a German-Jewish hit man for the LCN. His nickname was "Hole In The Head." Sources say he was respected and feared by many in the underworld and was known as a real capable guy—"capable," meaning that he would take one's head off in a heartbeat if he wanted to. He acted as a trusted go-between with Winter Hill and other gangs. (Courtesy of the Massachusetts State Police.)

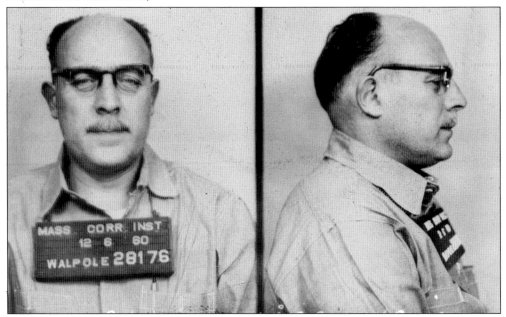

In the summer of 1960, Phil Waggenheim (above), Larry Zannino, and Leo A. Santaniello were accused of shaking down a North Shore construction company. On December 5, 1960, they pleaded guilty to charges of conspiracy and threatening injury to extort money. The *Boston Globe* reported that the district attorney requested high bail so the defendants "will not be able to silence their victims by burying them." (Courtesy of the Massachusetts State Police.)

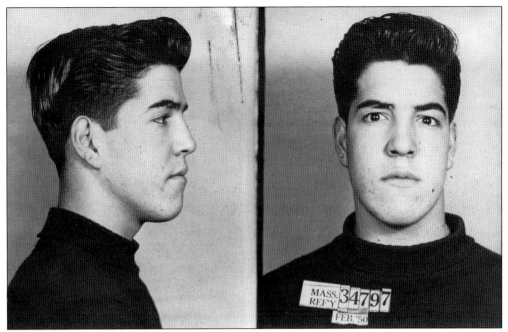

This fresh-faced youth with a wild look in his eye does not belong to a boy band. This is Joseph "The Animal" Barboza. Clean-cut and clean-shaven, the future hit man posed for this booking photograph in February 1950, not long after he and some pals got caught busting into houses around his hometown of New Bedford. In December 1949, the *Boston Herald Traveler* reported that Barboza's gang broke into over a dozen homes in New Bedford and "stole money, watches, liquor and guns." (Courtesy of the Massachusetts Department of Correction.)

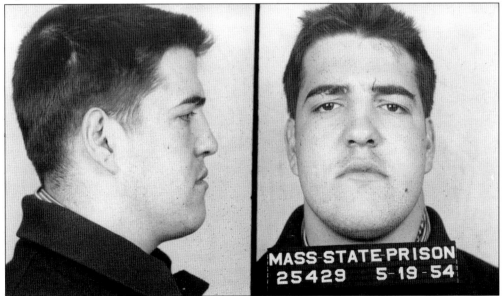

Barboza's former attorney, F. Lee Bailey, once said that Barboza "had no hesitation at all about describing the most cold-blooded, ruthless killings—he claimed more than 20, largely in the McLean-McLaughlin gang wars of the 1950s—as if he were eating a piece of apple pie." (Courtesy of the Massachusetts Department of Correction.)

Alvin Campbell (above), along with his brother Arnold Campbell and Dennis "Deke" Chandler (below), controlled Roxbury back in the day. These photographs were taken in 1968. In November of that year, Chandler and the Campbell brothers were accused of shooting and killing three people at the New England Grass Roots Organization (NEGRO) on Blue Hill Avenue. All three were found not guilty and were acquitted of murder charges. In 1970, Alvin Campbell was sentenced to 20 years in prison for selling cocaine. (Both, courtesy of the Massachusetts State Police.)

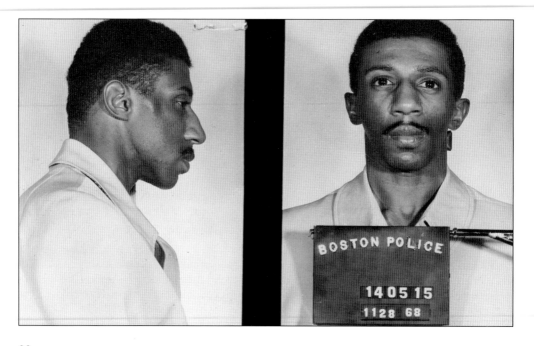

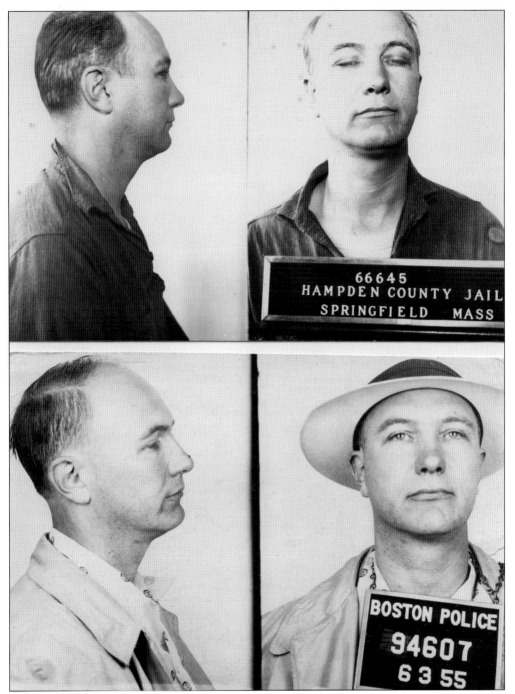

Edward A. "Wimpy" Bennett's eyes often appear to be closed—a distinctive trait that earned him his nickname because he resembled Popeye's hamburger-loving pal. Born on New Year's Day in 1919, he lived in Mattapan and was known to hang out with the Stephen "The Rifleman" Flemmi and his brother Jimmy "The Bear" Flemmi. Bennett was last seen alive in January 1967, wearing a black cashmere coat, grey felt hat, white shirt, and black shoes. (Courtesy of the Massachusetts State Police.)

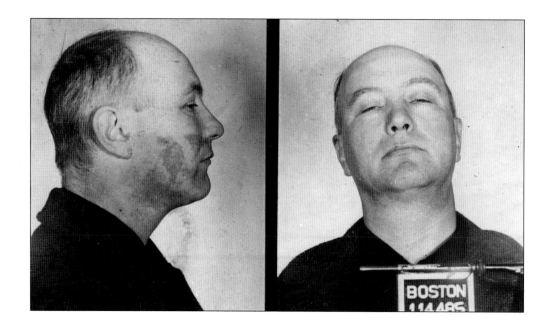

During the 1950s and 1960s, Edward A. "Wimpy" Bennett (above) and his brothers William and Walter were loan sharks and bookmakers who were viewed as Mafia rivals. The Bennett brothers all met untimely deaths—in January 1967, Wimpy Bennett disappeared; in April 1967, Walter Bennett disappeared; and on December 23, 1967, William Bennett was shot and thrown from a moving car into a snow bank. (Both, courtesy of the Massachusetts State Police.)

```
AU
-504                        63445
5049    FILE 6   PD BOSTON MASS   3-6-67
TO      APB
EDWARD A BENNET SR.      AKA "WIMPY    MASS RP-4314-A

MISSING FROM HIS HOME ON DIST 3 SINCE 11-00 AM OF 1-18-67
DESC AS W-M-47-5-11-185 GREY HAIR - BLUE EYES - FAIR COMP
WEARING BLACK CASHMERE COAT - GREY SUIT - GREY FELT HAT
WHITE SHIRT - BLACK SHOES - MAY BE OPER A 1966 CADILLAC
GREY WITH BLK VINYL TOP - MASS RP-4314-A OWNED BY CENTRAL
AUTO BODY - DULE / DUDLEY ST ROXBURY
HAS A HABIT OF ALWAYS CARRYING 2 BROWN SUT/ SUITCASES
IN TRUNK OF CAR - ABOVE SUBJECTS WIFE PASSED AWAY THIS  AM

AUTH LT HARTNETT  KUCHER   10-20 AM
RPB JFM 11-17 AM LINE A
```

025 505

NAME (Last name first)	NICKNAME OR ALIAS		GROUP	RANK	SEX	MBI#
Bennett, Edward A.	Wimpy				male	

ADDRESS*

CITY		TELEPHONE	

HGT.	WGT.	HAIR	EYES	DESCENT
5'10"		Grey	Hazel	

COMPLEXION, MARKS, SCARS, TATTOOS, ETC.

BIRTHDATE	TYPE ACTIVITY	FBI #
1-1-19		

SSN

ASSOCIATES
Stephen Joseph Vincent Flem[...]
VEHICLE(S) (*Year-make-body-type-colors-license no.*)

OCCUPATION	BUSINESS ADDRESS	CITY	BUSINESS PHONE

HANGOUTS
Sheriton Motor Inn - Neponset

MISC. INFO. (*additional addresses*)
See Ebb Tide

Form 21 — 2M-1-69-948775   INTELLIGENCE RECORD   DEPT. OF ATTORNEY GENERAL COMM. OF MASS.

BOSTON 129 312 11 17 65

Wimpy Bennett once lived on Hartford Street in Dorchester. His brother Walter owned Walter's Lounge on Dudley Street in Roxbury. Wimpy was also known to hang out at the Sheraton Motor Inn in the Neponset section of Dorchester, according to this police record. (Courtesy of the Massachusetts State Police.)

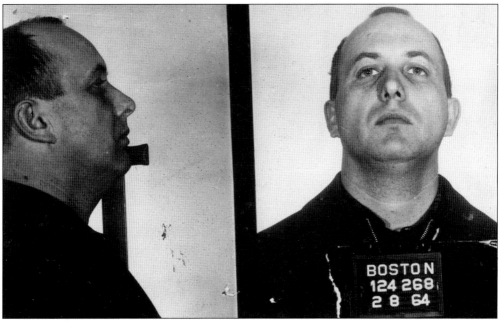

BOSTON 124 268 2 8 64

William O'Sullivan was a blue-eyed Marine from South Boston who went by the nickname "Billy O." He served as an enforcer for Donald Killeen, who ran gambling and bookmaking enterprises in South Boston. At one time he lived on Savin Hill Avenue in Dorchester. His listed occupation was bartender and longshoreman. He was murdered on March 28, 1971. (Courtesy of the Massachusetts State Police.)

This surveillance photograph shows bookmaker Donald Killeen. The *Boston Globe* called him the "boss of gambling in South Boston." The Killeen brothers often feuded with a group of Southie hoodlums known as the Mullen gang, who got their name from a square in South Boston dedicated to World War I veteran James Joseph Mullen. (It is located at the corner of O and East Second Streets.) In his memoir *A Criminal and an Irishman*, Patrick Nee described the Mullens as "wharf rats" who "mastered the art of tailgating off trucks loading and unloading at the warehouses by the waterfront." (Courtesy of the Massachusetts State Police.)

On May 13, 1972, Donald Killeen was shot to death outside his home on Edgell Road in Framingham. Killeen was 48 years old. Shortly after 9:00 p.m., he was ambushed and taken out with 15 shots fired from a submachine gun as he stepped outside during his son's birthday party. He was the third Killeen brother to die a violent death at the hand of gun. In 1950, his brother George was shot on Hanover Street in the North End. On June 9, 1955, Edward Killeen (also known as "The Gray Fox") was shot in the stomach as he was leaving the Transit Café. He never fully recovered from that gunshot wound, and he took his own life in 1968. (Courtesy of the Massachusetts State Police.)

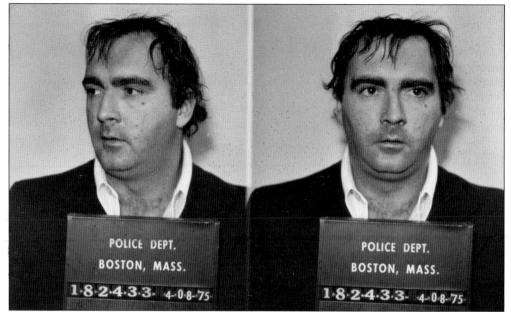

On May 11, 1982, Edward Brian Halloran (above) was getting a ride home from Michael Donahue, a truck driver from Dorchester. But neither man made it home. Halloran and Donahue were gunned down on Northern Avenue in South Boston. Halloran was 41 years old and had been living on Willard Street in Quincy. According to reports in the *Boston Globe*, Halloran had survived two previous attempts on his life over the past year and had recently decided to cooperate with the FBI against Bulger. (Courtesy of the Massachusetts State Police.)

On June 28, 1978, five men died in the cramped basement office of the Blackfriars Pub, located at 105 Summer Street in Boston. The victims of this gangland-style execution were pub manager John A. "Jack" Kelly, a former local television reporter; Blackfriars owner Vincent E. Solmonte, of Quincy; Peter F. Meroth, of Jamaica Plain; Charles G. Magarian, of North Andover; and Freddy R. Delavega, of Somerville. The case remains unsolved. (Courtesy of the *Boston Globe*; photograph by George Rizer.)

Seven

"THE ANIMAL" TAKES THE STAND

Edward Charles Deegan was a blue-eyed burglar who could break into anywhere. Everyone called him "Teddy." Born in January 1930, he grew up in Boston's West End and became a career hood. He was an accomplished burglar back when safecracking and lock-picking were highly respected skills within the underworld. (Courtesy of the Brookline Police Department.)

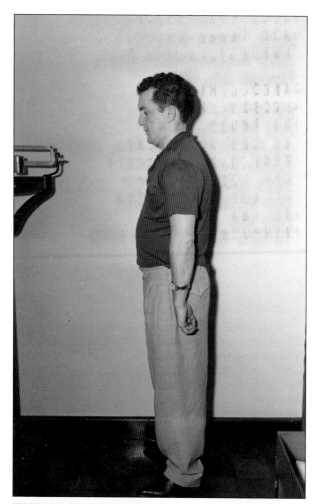

Deegan's criminal record went back to 1948, when he was arrested and charged with larceny as a teenager. Six years later, he was arrested again, on a charge of breaking and entering. He was also accused of several break-ins during the 1950s and 1960s. (Left, courtesy of the Brookline Police Department; below, courtesy of the Massachusetts State Police.)

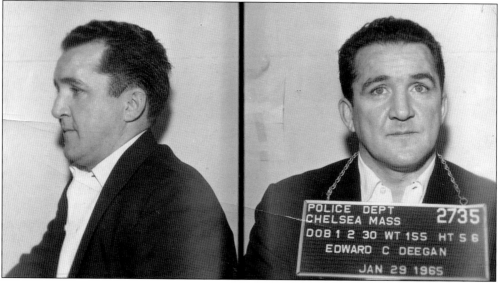

POLICE DEPT 2735
CHELSEA MASS
DOB 1 2 30 WT 155 HT 5 6
EDWARD C DEEGAN
JAN 29 1965

HC. 6248

NOV 13 1963 458

J. Edgar Hoover
Director.

The following FBI record, NUMBER 708 279 B , is furnished FOR OFFICIAL USE ONLY.

CONTRIBUTOR OF FINGERPRINTS	NAME AND NUMBER	ARRESTED OR RECEIVED	CHARGE	DISPOSITION
PD Boston Mass	Edward C Deegan #74464	2-22-48	SP Larceny Mdse over $100	
PD Boston Mass	Edward C Deegan #92342	8-29-54	SP B&E NT	
PD Boston Mass	Edward Charles Deegan #92342	10-13-55	SP-felonious A	
PD Boston Mass	Edward Charles Deegan #103141	5-11-58	SPL auto	
St Bu Boston Mass	Edward C Deegan #--	9-16-58	BE& L (daytime) open after susp	Dedham Dist Crt $5000 double surety
PD Boston Mass	Edward Charles Deegan #103,141	10-3-58	vio parole (A&B)	
Norfolk Co H of C Dedham Mass	Edward Charles Deegan #3827	6-26-59	B & E & L (DT)	6 mos
PD Boston Mass	Edward Charles Deegan #123327	10-22-63	SP-Armed Robbery	
PD Brookline Mass	Edward C. Deegan #3553	10-16-63	SP B&E	rel

Notations indicated by * ARE NOT BASED ON FINGERPRINTS IN FBI files. The notations are based on data formerly furnished this Bureau concerning individuals of the same or similar names or aliases and ARE LISTED ONLY AS INVESTIGATIVE LEADS.

16—70682-0 U. S. GOVERNMENT PRINTING OFFICE

In 1959, Deegan was sentenced to six months in the Norfolk County House of Correction. (Courtesy of the Brookline Police Department.)

Teddy Deegan's life was cut short after he was caught in a dark alley. On March 12, 1965, Deegan was gunned down as he attempted to break into this office building in Chelsea. The shooting took place at approximately 9:30 p.m. Police believed the shots were fired from three different weapons: one .45-caliber and two .38-caliber guns. (Courtesy of the Massachusetts State Police.)

Deegan was shot six times. He was found lying on his back near a doorway that provided access to the building at 375 Broadway. (Courtesy of the Massachusetts State Police.)

Deegan's body was found at approximately 11:00 p.m. in this back alley off Fourth Street in Chelsea. He was dressed in a suit, white shirt, and gloves. A 12-inch screwdriver was found on the ground near his left hand. (Courtesy of the Massachusetts State Police.)

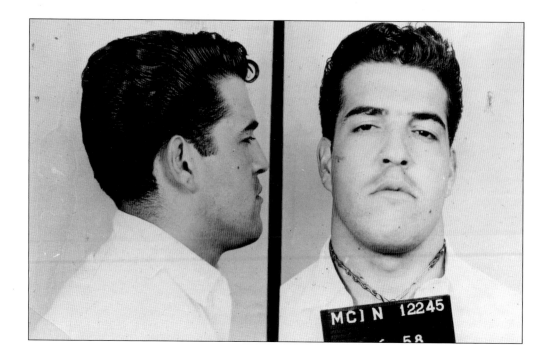

In the 1960s, Joseph "The Animal" Barboza (pictured above and below) agreed to become a cooperating witness against the Mafia. Barboza played a key role in the outcome of the Teddy Deegan murder case. He framed several of his rivals for Deegan's murder, and based on his false testimony, Peter Limone, Enrico "Henry" Tameleo, Louis Greco, and Joseph Salvati were convicted and sent to prison. (Both, courtesy of the Massachusetts State Police.)

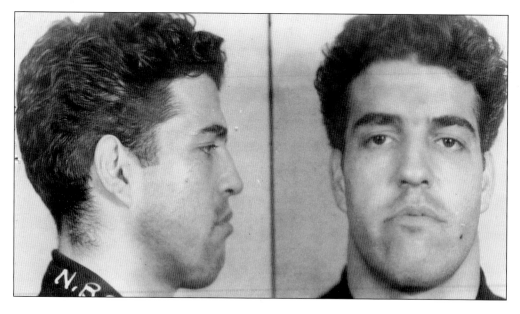

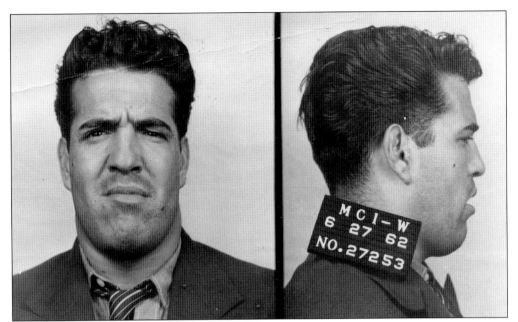

In 2007, US district court judge Nancy Gertner criticized how the FBI handled the Deegan case. "Even though the FBI knew Barboza's story was false, they encouraged him to testify in the Deegan murder trial," she said. "Indeed, they took steps to make certain that Barboza's false story would withstand cross-examination, and even be corroborated by other witnesses. In word and in deed, the FBI condoned Barboza's lies." (Courtesy of the Massachusetts Department of Correction.)

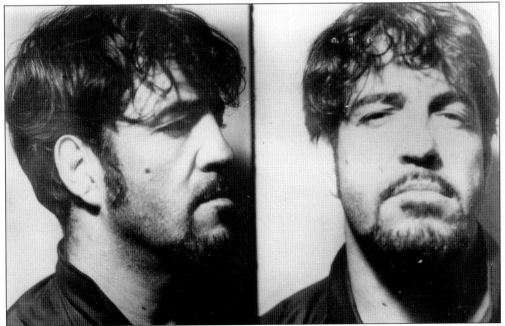

Barboza is widely recognized as being the first person to enter the federal witness protection program. After testifying against the Mafia in several trials, Barboza was relocated in April 1969 to Santa Rosa, California, where he took on a new identity and a new name (Joe Bentley) and enrolled in cooking school. (Courtesy of the Massachusetts State Police.)

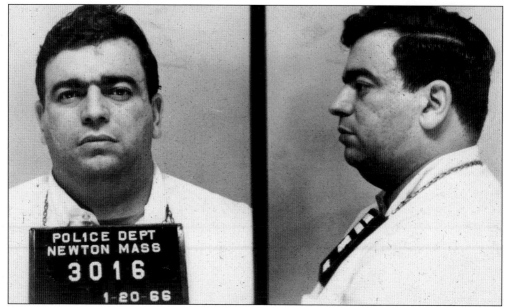

Ronald Cassesso was a reputed La Cosa Nostra soldier who participated in the Deegan murder. His nickname was "Ronnie the Pig." Cassesso was sent to prison in the 1960s for armed robbery. In 1967, Cassesso was indicted with Henry Tameleo and Raymond L.S. Patriarca on charges of conspiring to murder Willie Marfeo, who was shot and killed in a Providence restaurant on July 13, 1966. In 1968, Tameleo, Cassesso, and Patriarca were convicted on murder conspiracy charges, sentenced to five years in prison, and fined $10,000. (Courtesy of the Massachusetts State Police.)

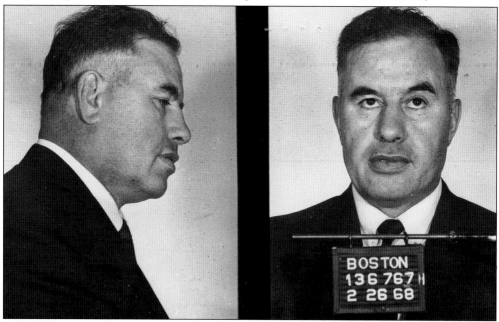

This booking photograph of Louis Greco was taken by the Boston Police Department in February 1968. A few months after this mug shot was taken, Greco was wrongfully convicted of Edward "Teddy" Deegan's murder. Greco died in prison in 1995 after serving 28 years for a crime he did not commit. (Courtesy of the Massachusetts State Police.)

BOTH THUMBS TAKEN TOGETHER	PRISONER'S SIGNATURE	*Louis Grieco*
	RESIDENCE	*21 Derby Road Revere Mass*

MOTHER'S NAME *Elizabeth* ?

FATHER'S NAME *Carman*

NAME **Lewis Grieco**   ALIASES **Louis Grieco**

CRIME *B & E to Com larceny*

COURT Suffolk Superior Court   DATE OF SENTENCE OCT 18 1935

SENTENCE Indeterminate, limited to 5 yrs.   HEIGHT *5* FT. *9* IN.   WEIGHT *140*

AGE *18*   EYES *dk blue*   BUILD *slender*

HAIR *cl blk*   OCCUPATION *junk dealer + laborer*

COMPLEXION *med fair*   DATE OF BIRTH *2/4/'17*

PLACE OF BIRTH *Revere Mass*

Here is Louis Greco in his younger days. In some early records, such as this one, his last name is spelled "Grieco." He was 18 years old when this photograph was taken in 1935, when he was sentenced on charges of breaking and entering. At the time, he lived in Revere. He went on to become a decorated World War II veteran. After he was framed by Barboza, he was sentenced to life in prison. Over time, his health deteriorated and he was unable to walk. During the final three months of his life, fellow inmate Joseph Salvati helped take care of him. (Courtesy of the Massachusetts State Police.)

This undated surveillance photograph shows Henry Tameleo (right), known in organized crime circles as "The Referee" who acted as an ambassador between Boston and Providence, chatting with Peter Fiumara (left), owner of the Squire Lounge, an adult entertainment venue in Revere. At the time this photograph was taken, Tameleo was on furlough from prison, where he was serving a life sentence for the murder of Edward "Teddy" Deegan. Tameleo died in prison in 1985 after serving 18 years for a crime he did not commit. (Courtesy of the Massachusetts State Police.)

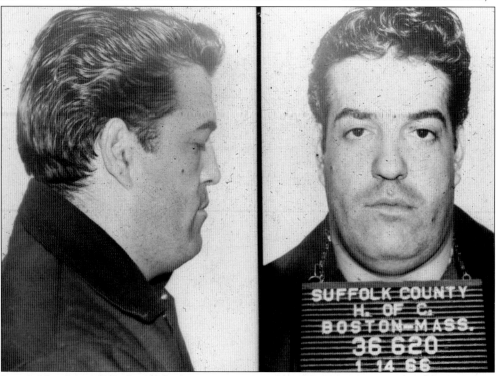

Joseph "the Animal" Barboza (also known as Joe Bentley or Joe Baron) was gunned down in San Francisco on February 11, 1976. On the afternoon he was killed, Barboza had just left his friend's apartment and was walking to his car, which was parked on the corner of Moraga Street and Twenty-fifth Avenue. (Courtesy of the Massachusetts Department of Correction.)

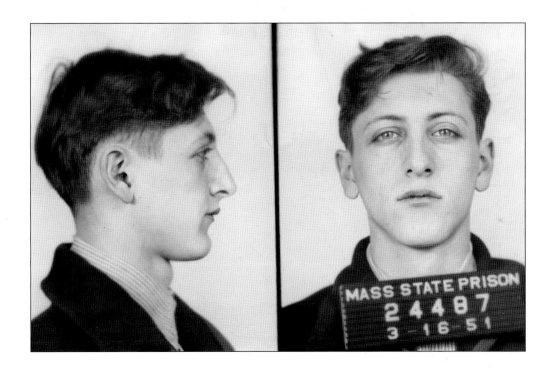

As Barboza approached his 1969 Ford Thunderbird, a white 1972 Ford Econoline van pulled up and stopped beside him. The cargo door on the right side of the van flew open and a man in a red ski cap—later identified as Joseph "J.R." Russo (pictured here)—opened fire with a shotgun. Russo ultimately did "The Animal" in. (Both, courtesy of the Massachusetts State Police.)

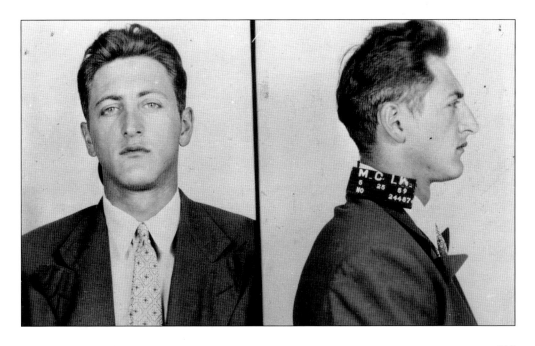

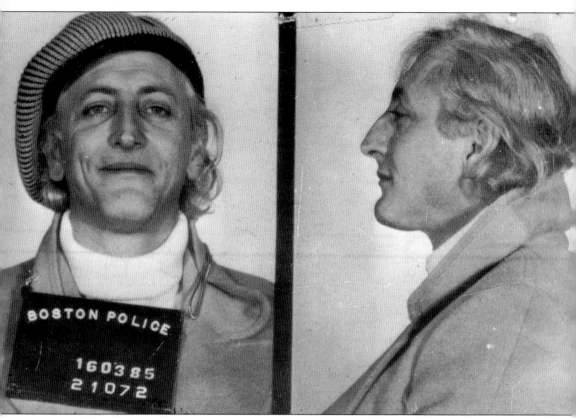

Joseph "J.R." Russo was believed to be a consigliere in the mob. He attended the infamous Mafia induction ceremony that was held in Medford in October 1989; the recording of that ceremony ultimately led to Russo's downfall. In 1992, Russo was convicted on racketeering charges and for the murder of Barboza. He was sentenced to 16 years in prison. Russo died from throat cancer in federal prison in Springfield, Missouri, in 1998; he was 67 years old. (Courtesy of the Massachusetts State Police.)

Eight

ON THE RUN

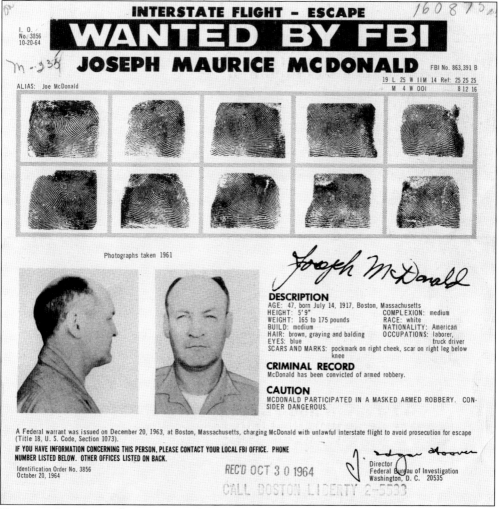

Known as "Joe Mac" in the streets, Joseph M. McDonald was a well-respected—and feared—member of the Winter Hill Gang in Somerville. In 1963, he escaped from prison while serving a 12-to-18-year sentence for armed robbery. (Courtesy of the Massachusetts State Police.)

Joe McDonald was born in July 1914. He was 46 years old when he made his prison escape in 1963. At the time, he stood five feet, nine inches tall and weighed between 165 and 175 pounds. He told authorities he made his living as a laborer and truck driver. (Courtesy of the Massachusetts State Police.)

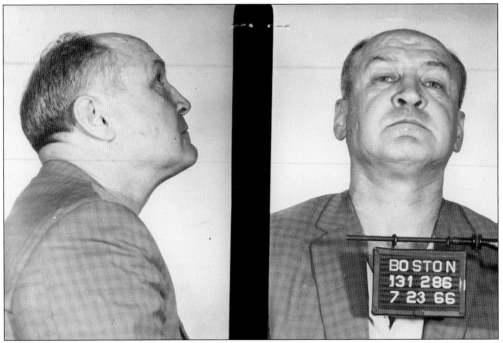

In 1976, the *Boston Globe* reported that McDonald made the FBI's 10 Most Wanted list in connection with the armed robbery of a stamp dealer on March 17, 1971. According to the *Globe,* a witness scheduled to testify in that case turned up dead. (Courtesy of the Massachusetts State Police.)

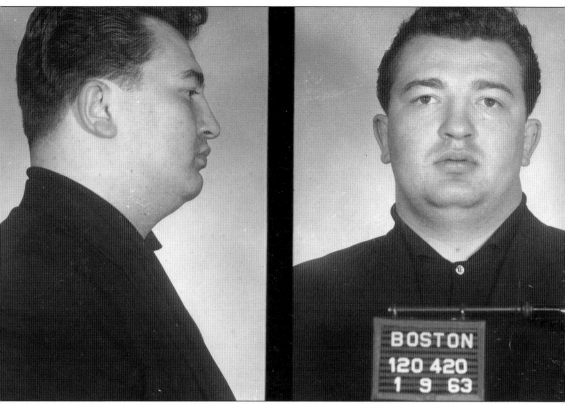

John Martorano was a hit man and longtime member of the Winter Hill Gang. He disappeared after he was indicted on federal racketeering charges in 1978. He remained a fugitive until 1995, when members of the Massachusetts State Police tracked him down in Florida. He was arrested there after being on the lam for 16 years. (Courtesy of the Massachusetts State Police.)

Martorano was indicted on racketeering charges related to the Winter Hill Gang's gambling, loan-sharking, and extortion operations. On September 30, 1999, Martorano pled guilty to charges related to 10 previously unsolved murders that occurred between 1973 and 1976. In June 2004, US district judge Mark L. Wolf sentenced the 63-year-old former hit man to 14 years in prison. (Courtesy of the Massachusetts State Police.)

Martorano cooperated with authorities and provided information that led to the convictions of former FBI agent John Connolly, former Massachusetts State Police lieutenant Richard Schneiderhan, and former FBI informant Stephen "The Rifleman" Flemmi. (Courtesy of the Massachusetts State Police.)

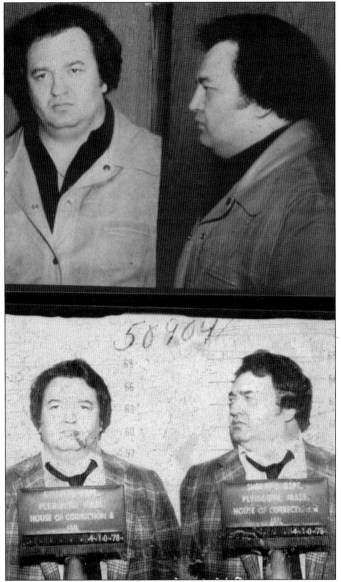

US attorney Michael J. Sullivan said Martorano's knowledge of underworld crime and corruption was key in solving these cases. "The unsavory reality for law enforcement is that we often have to deal with the worst kinds of criminals to get others in a criminal organization," said Sullivan in 2004. "Martorano's decision to cooperate literally opened the floodgates and led to, among other things, the cooperation of Kevin Weeks, Bulger's admitted 'right-hand man' and Frank Salemme, the leader of the mafia in New England. Weeks, Salemme and Martorano were essential to the Government in its attempt to fully unravel Bulger and Stephen J. "The Rifleman" Flemmi's criminal activity and to identify the extent of corruption within the Boston FBI at the time. Yet despite his extensive cooperation, the fact remains that Martorano is a criminal who committed numerous unspeakable acts of violence. My hope is that the victim families and the public understand the horrible dilemma we in law enforcement faced in this case and why John Martorano's cooperation was so important to the Government's investigation and why it was compelled to make this agreement." (Courtesy of the Massachusetts State Police.)

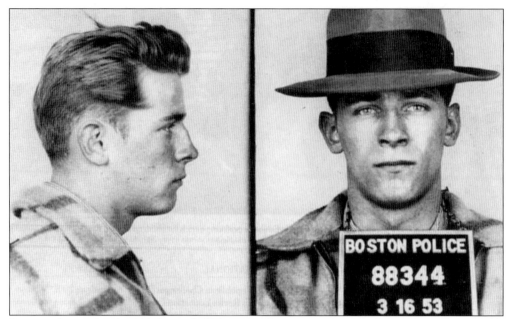

Born on September 3, 1929, James J. "Whitey" Bulger grew up in South Boston and eventually became one of the most notorious organized crime figures in the country. This Boston police booking photograph was taken in 1953. (Courtesy of the *Boston Globe*.)

This photograph shows Alcatraz prison around the time James J. "Whitey" Bulger was incarcerated there. Bulger entered Alcatraz on November 13, 1959, and was identified as Inmate No. 1428. He spent three years behind bars there for taking part in a bank robbery. (Author's collection.)

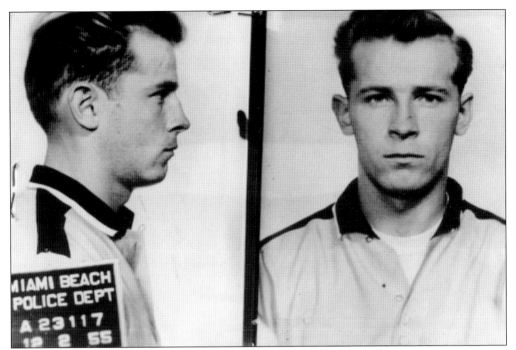

This mug shot of Whitey Bulger was taken by the Miami Beach Police Department in 1955. (Courtesy of the *Boston Globe*.)

Once upon a time, Whitey Bulger lived at this sea-green condominium development on West Fourth Street in South Boston. In the late 1980s, Bulger had a condo at 327 West Fourth Street, and his right-hand man, Kevin Weeks, lived next door at 329 West Fourth Street. (Photograph by Emily Sweeney.)

Triple O's Lounge was located at 28 West Broadway in South Boston. It was a dive bar—kind of dark, with low ceilings, a small dance floor, a pool table, and long mirrors on the walls; the type of place where hot dogs were served from a lit-up rotating grill at the bar. It was also the place where Whitey Bulger and his associates allegedly shook down bookies and collected unpaid loans. In 1990, Triple O's was raided by the feds, who were searching for evidence to use against Bulger. Triple O's owner, Kevin P. O'Neil, later agreed to cooperate against Bulger and pleaded guilty to racketeering, money laundering, and extortion charges. O'Neil was sentenced to one year and one day in prison. The shady bar known as Triple O's is now long gone. Today, 28 Broadway is home to an upscale Asian bistro. (Photograph by Emily Sweeney.)

FBI TEN MOST WANTED FUGITIVE

Racketeering Influenced and Corrupt Organizations (RICO) - Murder (19 Counts),
Conspiracy to Commit Murder, Conspiracy to Commit Extortion, Narcotics
Distribution, Conspiracy to Commit Money Laundering; Extortion; Money Laundering

JAMES J. BULGER

| Photograph | Photograph Age | Photograph Age |
| taken in 1994 | Enhanced in 2008 | Enhanced in 2008 |

Aliases:
Thomas F. Baxter, Mark Shapeton, Jimmy Bulger, James Joseph Bulger, James J. Bulger, Jr., James Joseph Bulger, Jr.,
Tom Harris, Tom Marshall, Ernest E. Beaudreau, Harold W. Evers, Robert William Hanson, "Whitey"

DESCRIPTION

Date(s) of Birth Used:	September 3, 1929	Hair:	White/Silver
Place of Birth:	Boston, Massachusetts	Eyes:	Blue
Height:	5'7" to 5'9"	Complexion:	Light
Weight:	150 to 160 pounds	Sex:	Male
Build:	Medium	Race:	White
Occupation:	Unknown	Nationality:	American

Scars and Marks: None known
Remarks: Bulger is an avid reader with an interest in history. He is known to frequent libraries and historic sites. Bulger may be taking heart medication. He maintains his physical fitness by walking on beaches and in parks with his female companion, Catherine Elizabeth Greig . Bulger and Greig love animals. Bulger has been known to alter his appearance through the use of disguises. He has traveled extensively throughout the United States, Europe, Canada, and Mexico.

CAUTION

James J. Bulger is being sought for his role in numerous murders committed from the early 1970s through the mid-1980s in connection with his leadership of an organized crime group that allegedly controlled extortion, drug deals, and other illegal activities in the Boston, Massachusetts, area. He has a violent temper and is known to carry a knife at all times.

REWARD

The FBI is offering a $2,000,000 reward for information leading directly to the arrest of James J. Bulger.

CONSIDERED ARMED AND EXTREMELY DANGEROUS

If you have any information concerning this person, please contact your local FBI office or the nearest American Embassy or Consulate.
August 1999 Poster Revised September 2008

Bulger made it onto the FBI's 10 Most Wanted list in 1999. The FBI offered a $2-million reward—the largest ever offered for a domestic fugitive. On June 22, 2011, Bulger and his girlfriend, Catherine E. Greig, were apprehended in California. The couple had been living on the run since 1995. They had been living under fake names—Charlie and Carol Gasko—at a rent-controlled apartment at 1012 Third Street in Santa Monica. Their rent was $1,165 a month. Authorities searched the apartment and found guns, knives, and over $800,000 in cash as well as a book entitled *Secrets of a Back-Alley ID Man: Fake ID Construction Techniques of the Underground* by Sheldon Charrett. At the time of their arrests, Bulger was 81 years old and Greig was 60 years old. (Courtesy of the Federal Bureau of Investigation.)

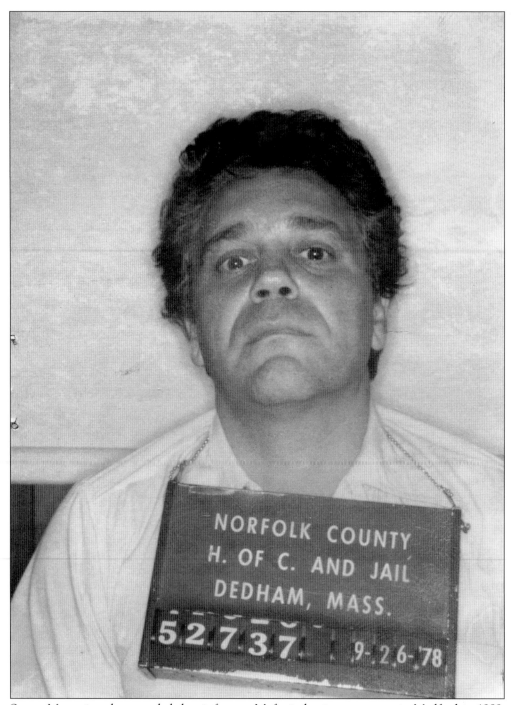

Sonny Mercurio, who attended that infamous Mafia induction ceremony in Medford in 1989, was also known to skip town before indictments were unsealed. According to the *Boston Herald*, he once said: "Power of the lam means you get a lesser sentence. I advocate everybody run away." (Courtesy of the Massachusetts State Police.)

BIBLIOGRAPHY

Carr, Howie. *Hitman: The Untold Story of Johnny Martorano*. New York, NY: Forge, 2011.

Commonwealth v. Anthony Demboski and another. 283 Mass. 315. Suffolk County. (May 12, May 15–June 26, 1933.)

Commonwealth of Massachusetts v. George P. McLaughlin. 352 Mass. 218. Suffolk County. (Supreme Judicial Court of Massachusetts. March 9, 1967.)

Investigation of Improper Activities in the Labor or Management Field. Hearings before select committee on Improper Activities in the Labor or Management Field. 85th Congress, first session. US Government Printing Office, Washington, DC: 1958.

Investigation of Organized Crime in Interstate Commerce. United States Senate, Special Committee to Investigate Organized Crime in Interstate Commerce. 1950.

Litif v. United States, John Morris, and John Connolly. (US District Court, District of Massachusetts. Civil Action No. 02-11791-WGY.)

Martini, Bobby, and Elayne Keratsis. *Citizen Somerville: Growing up with the Winter Hill Gang*. North Reading, MA: Powder House Press, 2010.

Nee, Patrick, Richard Farrell, and Michael Blythe. *A Criminal and An Irishman: The Inside Story of the Boston Mob–IRA Connection*. Hanover, NH: Steerforth Press, 2006.

O'Neill, Gerard, and Dick Lehr. *The Underboss: The Rise and Fall of a Mafia Family*. Cambridge, MA: PublicAffairs, 1989.

———. *Black Mass: The Irish Mob, the FBI, and a Devil's Deal*. Cambridge, MA: PublicAffairs, 2000.

Peter J. Limone et al v. United States of America. (US District Court, District of Massachusetts. Civil Action No. 02cv10890-NG.)

Ranalli, Ralph. *Deadly Alliance: The FBI's Secret Partnership With the Mob*. New York, NY: HarperCollins, 2001.

Weeks, Kevin, and Phyllis Karas. *Brutal: The Untold Story of My Life Inside Whitey Bulger's Irish Mob*. New York, NY: HarperCollins, 2006.

United States of America v. Francis P. Salemme, James J. Bulger, Stephen J. Flemmi, Robert P. Deluca, James M. Martorano v. District Court of Massachusetts. 4th Superseding Indictment. (1996.)

United States Congressional Serial Set, Serial No. 14913, House Report No. 414, "Everything Secret Degenerates: The FBI's Use of Murderers as Informants, Vol. 2."

DISCOVER THOUSANDS OF LOCAL HISTORY BOOKS
FEATURING MILLIONS OF VINTAGE IMAGES

Arcadia Publishing, the leading local history publisher in the United States, is committed to making history accessible and meaningful through publishing books that celebrate and preserve the heritage of America's people and places.

Find more books like this at
www.arcadiapublishing.com

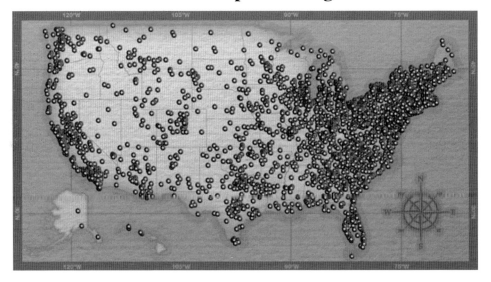

Search for your hometown history, your old stomping grounds, and even your favorite sports team.

Consistent with our mission to preserve history on a local level, this book was printed in South Carolina on American-made paper and manufactured entirely in the United States. Products carrying the accredited Forest Stewardship Council (FSC) label are printed on 100 percent FSC-certified paper.

MADE IN THE USA